BESSER IN ENGLISCH

GRAMMATIK 5./6. SCHULJAHR

von David Clarke und Ingrid Preedy

Band I

Cornelsen
SCRIPTOR

Besser in Englisch, Grammatik für das 5./6. Schuljahr, Band I,
wurde geplant und entwickelt von der Cornelsen & Oxford University Press GmbH, Berlin, im Auftrag des Scriptor Verlages, Frankfurt am Main.

Verfasser David Clarke und Ingrid Preedy
Beratende Mitwirkung Helga Clarke

CIP-Titelaufnahme der Deutschen Bibliothek

Besser in Englisch. – Frankfurt am Main: Cornelsen Scriptor
(Scriptor Lernhilfen)
Grammatik / David Clarke; Ingrid Preedy.
Schuljahr 5/6. – 1989
Band 1. – 1989
ISBN 3-589-20880-5

1. Auflage

7.	6.	5.	4.	Die letzten Ziffern bezeichnen Zahl
1997	96	95	94	und Jahr des Druckes.

Veröffentlichung der deutschen Ausgabe bei Cornelsen Verlag Scriptor, Frankfurt am Main.

Dieser Lernhilfe ist ein Lösungsheft zu den Übungen beigefügt.

Verlagsredaktion Christopher A. Caridia und James Abram

Illustrationen Caroline Ewen, Hewett Street Studios, London und Christine Georg, Dortmund
Umschlaggestaltung Studio Lochmann, Frankfurt am Main

Satz Fotosatz Gleißberg & Wittstock, Berlin
Druck Adolph Fürst & Sohn, Berlin

Vertrieb Cornelsen Verlag, Berlin

ISBN 3-589-20880-5

BESSER IN ENGLISCH

GRAMMATIK 5./6. SCHULJAHR

Lösungsheft

Band I

Cornelsen
SCRIPTOR

1 Das Verb *be*

❶ (is) – am – is – are – are – am – is – is – am – is – is

❷ 1 (was) – was 2 were – were 3 was – was – was
4 were – was

❸ 1 is
2 were – were – were
3 was – was – was – is – are
4 is – am – was – are – are – am – am

❹ 2 are not (aren't)
3 is not (isn't)
4 are not (aren't)
5 were not (weren't)
6 was not (wasn't)
7 am not ('m not)

❺ 2 Is Tom often late for school?
3 Was Bob captain last year?
4 Are Sally and Bob good friends?
5 Were Tom and Sally at Bob's party?
6 Am I in the team for the next match?

❻ 2 Don't be – Be helpful
3 Don't be – Be good
4 Don't be so silly – Be sensible
5 Don't be so careless, Freddy. Be careful, please.

❼ 2 Are the Cobb children ... ?
3 Is Old Carter ... ?
4 Is Spooky ... ?
5 Am I ... ?
6 Are Hamburg and Cologne ... ?
7 Was Bob Pratt ... ?
8 Were the bikes ... ?

❽ (It's) – They're – Where's – there's – They're – That's – isn't it – Coke's – you're – He's – What's – We're

❾ *Tom* (Miss Jolly's) – Mr Carter isn't – He's
Sally Old Carter's – You're – that's – You're – you're – I'm – he's
Bob Sally's – you weren't – you weren't

Puzzle page

1 a pop star (A) 2 Edinburgh (B) 3 Italy (E) 4 flowers (R) 5 London (D)
6 Ireland (E) 7 Elizabeth II (E) 8 pop singers (N)
The town is ABERDEEN.

2 Das Verb *have*

1
1 (have got) – has got – (has) – has got – has – has
2 *Mr Carter*: have *Tom:* have got *Mr. Carter*: have got – have got
3 has – have – has – has got – has

2
1 (had) – had
2 had – had
3 had – had got – had got

3
1 have got – has – has got
2 had – had – had – had
3 had – had – have – have got – have got – had – have got – have

4
1 Has Tom Cobb got ... ? – has not got (hasn't got)
2 Have Tom and Sally got ... ? – have not got (haven't got)
3 Does Elvira have ... ? – does not (doesn't) have some milk
4 Do Bob and Tom have ... ? – do not (don't) have a good time at the youth club every week
5 Do you have ... ? – do not (don't) have
6 Have ... got some felt-tip pens? – I have not (haven't) got any felt-tip pens.

5
1 Elvira did not (didn't) have – Did Elvira have ... ?
2 Sally and Tom did not (didn't) have – Did Sally and Tom have ... ?
3 Bob did not (didn't) have – Did Bob have ... ?
4 Prof. Hudd did not (didn't) have an accident – Did Prof. Hudd have an accident ... ?
5 I did not (didn't) have a good time at the weekend. – Did you have a good time at the weekend?

6
3 The Romans did not have
4 Have the Cobbs got
5 Bob has not (hasn't) got
6 Did Robin Hood have
7 Has Mr Carter got
8 The old Greeks didn't have
9 Elvira hasn't got
10 Did ... have

Puzzle page

(three apples), two oranges, five strawberries, two bananas, four potatoes, four tomatoes, one cabbage, and six carrots ...

3 Das Verb *do*

1
1 does 2 did 3 do 4 does 5 did 6 did 7 do
8 does

2

3 Do the children live ... ? – do
4 Did Spooky go ... ? – didn't
5 Did Green Park win ... ? – didn't
6 Does Freddy eat ... ? Yes, he does.
7 Did Mr Carter get angry ... ? No, he didn't.
8 Does Elvira help her mother a lot? Yes, she does.
9 Did Tom and Sally buy some new jeans on Saturday? No, they didn't.

3

2 does not work – works
3 does not like – likes
4 do not live – live
5 does not eat – eats
6 does not go out with Mr Taylor. She goes out with Mr Carter.
7 do not watch videos at the weekend. They play games and read.

4

1 Does Elvira live ... ?
2 British children do not (don't) go
3 we did not (didn't) go
4 Do Tom and Bob play ... ?
5 Do the children help ... ?
6 Do you like reading ... ?

5

2 Don't feed
3 Don't swim
4 Don't throw bottles
5 Don't smoke
6 Don't play
7 Don't play football
8 Don't pick the flowers

6

2 Does Tom do ... ? – he does.
3 Do the Cobbs do ... ? – they do.
4 Do Bob and Tom do ... ? – they don't.
5 Did Freddy do the washing-up last night? – he didn't.
6 Do Tom and Sally do their English together? – they do.

7

2 do the gardening ... ?
3 Does Bob do his homework ... ?
4 Tom and Sally did not (didn't) do the shopping
5 Does Miss Jolly do her hair ... ?
6 Elvira does not (doesn't) do her bed
7 Did the boys and girls do a Maths test ... ?
8 We did two jigsaw puzzles
9 Freddy does not (doesn't) do the washing-up

Puzzle page

DOctor – **DO**g – **DO**ll – **DO**lphin – **DO**mino – **DO**nkey – **DO**or – **DO**wn

4 Die Fragewörter

❶
3 When does Elvira get up?
4 Why are ... late?
5 What does Sally give Tweets every morning?
6 Who did ... see at the youth club disco yesterday?
7 Where is the post office?
8 How do you switch on the cooker?

❷ 2 Who ... ? 3 Who ... ? 4 What ... ? 5 Who ... ? 6 What ... ?

❸
2 Why is Miss Jolly angry?
3 What happened at work today?
4 What did ... do yesterday?
5 Who danced with Tom at Elvira's party?
6 Who does Elvira love?
7 When do ... have lunch?
8 How do you do that sum?
9 Where does Elvira Nunn live?

❹ 2 Whose bird is ... ? 3 Whose form teacher is ... ?
4 Whose neighbour is ... ?

Puzzle page

(von oben) 5 – 9 – 2 – 10 – 11 – 4 – 8 – 3 – 7 – (1) – 6

5 Das *simple present*

❶ (live) – have – go – works – drives – needs – play – go – come – stay – bring – likes.

❷ (he likes) – she cries – it cuts – she dresses – he finds – it flies – he pushes – she swims – they teach – I wash – she eats – he goes

❸ gets up – eats – catches – works – goes – washes – makes – finishes – rings up – talks – watches – reads – writes

❹
2 always comes home from school at 4 o'clock.
3 buys a comic on Saturdays.
4 often listens to records.
5 never walks to school.
7 always go to school by bus.
8 play basketball on Saturdays.
9 often meet their friends.
10 never do the cooking.

5
2 doesn't sell apples.
3 doesn't drink lemonade.
4 don't run to school.
5 I don't speak French.
6 doesn't love Jim.
7 they don't sleep at night.
8 she doesn't make cakes.

6
2 Does Mr Carter come ... ?
3 Do ... live ... ?
4 Do the boys always run ... ?
5 Has Elvira got ... ?
6 Can the Queen go ... ?
7 Does Bob often write a postcard ... ?

7
2 My father works in London.
3 He never listens to pop records.
4 Do fish live in water?
5 Does Dirk's sister sometimes help him with his homework?
6 Colin often writes to his grandmother in Canada.
7 We don't watch a lot of TV at the weekend.
8 The supermarket doesn't sell English books.
9 Do dogs sleep at night?

Puzzle page

1 go
2 see
3 has
4 gets
5 looks
6 works
7 must go
8 starts
9 is
10 takes
11 goes
12 comes
13 watches
14 meet
15 go
16 have
17 has
18 does

(Ness war's natürlich!)

6 Das *present progressive*

1
1 (is doing) – is helping – are cutting
2 are tidying up – is putting – is making
3 am watching
4 am having – am ('m) writing – is swimming – is running – is barking – are sleeping

2
1 Bob is scoring a goal.
2 Tweets is singing in her cage.
3 Elvira is running to the bus-stop.
4 Sally and Bob are practising a new dance.
5 Mrs Cobb is making a bed.
6 Freddy Clarke is sleeping in bed.

❸
1 I am playing with my little dog.
2 Tom is repairing his bike.
3 My parents are sleeping. Please be quiet.
4 I am tidying up my room.
5 We are helping our parents in the kitchen.

❹
2 are not waiting
3 is not cleaning
4 are not listening
5 am not making
6 are not putting away your

❺
2 Are you helping ... ?
3 Is Elvira wearing ... ?
4 Are Miss Jolly and Mr Carter sitting ... ?
5 Am I playing ... ?
6 Are we doing a German test now?
7 Is Freddy eating toffees again?

❻
Sally am standing – am talking
Elvira –
Sally am doing – Are you doing ... ?
Elvira am trying – am finding
Sally is listening
Elvira Are they practising ... ?
Sally are making – is trying – is barking – are playing
Elvira Are you going ... ?
Sally –

❼
1 (is winning) – is not running – is – runs – think – is not trying – are – is – wants
2 Are you tidying – are you playing ... ? – am tidying – play – put
3 is not doing – is becoming – does – forgets – does not wear – comes – is getting

Puzzle page

1/E – 2/L – 3/I – 4/Z – 5/A – 6/B – 7/E – 8/T – 9/H (ELIZABETH)

7 Das *simple past*

❶ (was) – (phoned) – happened – wanted to – fetched – put – climbed – helped – happened – dropped – shouted – fell – called – came – looked at – said – drove
regelmäßig: (phone, phoned) – happen, happened – want to, wanted to – fetch, fetched – climb, climbed – help, helped – drop, dropped – shout, shouted – call, called – look at, looked at
unregelmäßig: (be, was) – put, put – fall, fell – come, came – say, said – drive, drove

❷ 2 rained – stayed – played 3 saw 4 came 5 bought
6 knew 7 went – was 8 did – was 9 wrote 10 saw

❸ 2 Did Mr Carter take a bus?
3 Did Miss Jolly buy a dress?
4 Did Bob go to bed at nine o'clock?
5 Did Sally do the washing-up?
6 Did Elvira clean her room?
7 Did Tom repair his bicycle?
8 Did Mrs Nunn have a day's holiday?

❹ 2 Where did Tom go to ... ?
3 What did ... play ... ?
4 did Spooky run after ... ?
5 What did ... watch ... ?
6 Who did Elvira see on Monday?
7 did Sally catch a cold?

❺ 2 didn't phone the police.
3 didn't run in front of the car.
4 didn't come too quickly.
5 didn't stop in time.
6 didn't come to the accident.
7 didn't take a taxi.

❻ 1 Yesterday our uncle came – He gave
2 Did you go to the cinema two days ago? – I didn't go – I went
3 Elvira danced – But she didn't win.
4 Miss Jolly and Mr Carter met (each other) – Tom saw them

Puzzle page

(von oben) 3 – 8 – (1) – 10 – 2 – 6 – 4 – 9 – 7 – 11 – 5

8 Das *past progressive*

❶
2 was tidying up
3 were swimming
4 was going to
5 were working
6 was making – was watching TV
7 Bob and Tom were playing with Spooky.

❷
1 walked – were sitting – were reading – were doing – were talking – was planning – was eating – ate
2 saw – was coming – started – tried – missed – hit – was driving – was – was sitting – went – was writing – was laughing

❸
2 was not (wasn't) doing – was doing the cleaning.
3 were not (weren't) cleaning – were cleaning the windows.
4 was not (wasn't) practising – was practising the piano.
5 were not (weren't) being – were working
6 were not (weren't) doing – were having

❹
2 When was Sally learning ... ?
3 Where were Bob and Elvira dancing ... ?
4 Who was helping Miss Jolly ... ?
5 What were you doing ... ?
6 When was Mrs Nunn working till ... ?

❺
1 was not (wasn't) playing – was practising
2 are you talking ... ?
3 were camping
4 were not (weren't) baking – were making
5 Was she laughing ... ? – was telling
6 were not (weren't) being – were playing
7 Were you doing ... ?
8 were you doing ... ? – was taking
9 was not (wasn't) looking – was going – was teasing

Puzzle page

Billy	was having
Fred / wife	were reading
Larry	was phoning
Peter	was watching
Sally	was drinking
Sam	was playing
Cat / Dirty	were walking
Bessy	was talking
Mack	was cooking

(The thief was) Sam Short (because) Bessy and Larry both say that they were phoning each other.

9 Das *present perfect*

1 (I've worked) – you haven't finished – I haven't finished – I've washed – I've mended – I've cleaned – Haven't I done ... ? – you haven't taken – you haven't written – you haven't thanked – It's rained – I haven't been – you haven't done – (Bob and I) have learnt

2
1 has gone
2 have been
3 has fed
4 have not (haven't) done
5 has given
6 have eaten
7 have made
8 have told

3
2 They have (They've) done their homework.
3 He has (He's) bought a new car.
4 They have (They've) finished the garden.
5 He has (He's) eaten too many toffees.
6 have been on holiday.

4
2 have already done
3 have not yet finished
4 Have ... ever seen ... ?
5 has never been
6 have just bought
7 Have ... already seen ... ?
8 has already eaten

5 1 bought 2 has just had 3 have you done 4 bought 5 went
6 have never run

6
1 went – met – asked – have seen – saw – was – have not seen – said – saw – was – have won – has given
2 have you seen ... ? – have not seen – saw – went

Puzzle page

T	H	G	U	A	T	F	A	T	Q	I	O	U	B	J
C	V	A	C	A	U	G	H	T	R	D	C	L	E	E
G	C	H	B	B	R	K	V	U	R	I	F	D	G	W
E	Q	T	U	F	P	L	E	N	T	C	D	B	Q	P
S	N	I	S	E	K	G	Z	T	R	N	O	D	X	N
O	L	G	X	H	S	B	A	D	E	O	N	M	E	Y
T	W	R	A	E	O	B	Q	K	Z	L	E	D	M	N
L	E	Z	Y	E	B	E	E	N	T	M	E	A	N	T
P	A	H	I	Y	T	G	S	O	N	L	Y	I	Z	O
M	T	F	U	X	C	U	T	W	X	C	H	D	E	R
G	E	R	Y	B	L	N	I	N	D	X	X	O	G	M
I	N	H	Q	P	J	L	O	M	H	R	P	G	R	A
K	V	B	E	N	A	J	W	I	V	A	A	C	O	W
K	U	G	B	U	J	D	P	H	Q	B	U	W	W	L
N	E	T	T	O	G	R	O	F	S	K	I	D	N	A

10 Das *going to-* und das *will-future*

❶
2 is going to dance
3 is going to play
4 are going to work
5 are going to decorate
6 is going to drive

❷
2 will rain
3 will not (won't) play
4 will be
5 will not (won't) come – will get
6 will miss

❸
3 will be
4 am not going to buy – am going to give
5 will get
6 will not (won't) bark
7 will be – will die
8 is going to give
9 will be
10 are going to get

Puzzle page

2 shopkeeper.
3 be a dancer.
4 mechanics.
5 is going to be a taxi-driver.
6 is going to be a vet.
7 nurses.
8 is going to be a star footballer.
9 is going to be a dentist.

11 Modale Hilfsverben

❶
1 (can't speak) – bake – swim – can drive – repair
2 can't speak – repair – can drive – bake – swim.

❷
2 can – Could he swim ... ? – couldn't
3 he can – Could he roller-skate ... ? – couldn't
4 she can – Could she read German ... ? – couldn't
5 can – Could you ride a bike ... ? – I couldn't

❸
1 mustn't
2 must
3 mustn't – must
4 mustn't
5 mustn't – must
6 mustn't – must

❹
2 mustn't
3 must (have to)
4 must (have to) – mustn't
5 must (have to)
6 needn't (don't have to)
7 mustn't – needn't (don't have to)

❺
2 can help – mustn't feed
3 mustn't swim – can have
4 must (have to) be – needn't (don't have to) go
5 must drive – needn't (don't have to) use
6 mustn't go – can wait

Puzzle page

Freie Lösung

Little Red Riding Hood

1 was 2 lived 3 wore 4 use / used 5 call
6 said 7 is 8 is lying 9 needs 10 take 11 be
12 is waiting 13 put on 14 picked up 15 kissed 16 left
17 will go 18 thought 19 is / will be 20 went
21 was walking 22 came 23 spoke 24 said
25 are you going 26 am taking 27 answered 28 is
29 is lying 30 must hurry 31 is feeling 32 is waiting
33 heard 34 felt 35 looked at 36 had 37 said 38 ran
39 arrived 40 opened 41 went 42 laid 43 climbed
44 knocked 45 called 46 pushed 47 went 48 thought
49 looked 50 seemed 51 said 52 are you feeling / do you feel
53 am not feeling / don't feel 54 said 55 are you standing
56 Come 57 moved 58 looked 59 have 60 said
61 jumped 62 caught 63 ate
64 left 65 went 66 was 67 wanted
68 became 69 wonder 70 has happened 71 thought
72 has been 73 has lost 74 will go 75 find 76 will know
77 heard 78 said 79 know 80 has happened 81 has eaten
82 don't worry 83 will shoot 84 is not / won't be 85 got
86 went 87 found 88 killed 89 took 90 cut
91 climbed 92 looked 93 were

1. Auflage
7. 6. 5. 4. | Die letzten Ziffern bezeichnen
1997 96 95 94 | Zahl und Jahr des Druckes.

Veröffentlichung der deutschen Ausgabe bei Scriptor Verlag, Frankfurt am Main.

Inhaltsverzeichnis

Möchtest du besser in Englisch werden?

Warst du in letzter Zeit mal krank und hast deswegen ein paar Englischstunden versäumt? Fühlst du dich bei Klassenarbeiten manchmal unsicher? Hast du vielleicht auch einiges schon wieder vergessen – oder von Anfang an gar nicht richtig verstanden?

Ganz egal aus welchem Grund du Schwierigkeiten hast, dieses Buch wird dir helfen, dein Englisch zu verbessern!

Hier sind ein paar Tips wie du am besten mit *Besser in Englisch* arbeiten solltest:

♦ Das **Inhaltsverzeichnis** zeigt dir, was in den einzelnen Kapiteln angeboten wird. Du kannst das ganze Buch von vorne bis hinten durcharbeiten, oder die Themen heraussuchen, die du gerade nacharbeiten möchtest.

♦ Der **Computerbildschirm** am Anfang jedes Kapitels zeigt dir alle Themen, die in dem Kapitel vorkommen. Das hilft dir auch, genau das Richtige für dich herauszusuchen.

♦ Die **Erklärungen** sind immer gleich aufgebaut. Die **Beispielsätze** zeigen dir, was in dem Abschnitt behandelt wird. Du solltest sie immer ganz gründlich durchlesen. Dann wird die Form vorgestellt und anschließend wird erklärt, wie man sie verwendet. Nimm dir immer genügend Zeit, damit du die Erklärungen auch richtig verstehst. Die Nummern im Kästchen beziehen sich auf die Beispielsätze.

♦ '**Ness**' soll dir bei besonderen Schwierigkeiten helfen!

♦ **Die Übungen** am Anfang jedes Kapitels sind einfach, werden aber zunehmend schwieriger!

♦ Der **Bleistift** sagt dir, daß es sich hier um eine Übung handelt, in der nur eine einzige Form eines grammatischen Themas vorkommt.

♦ Das **Auto** markiert eine schwierige Übung, in der alle Formen und Verwendungen des Themas gemischt und durcheinander abgefragt werden, genau wie bei Klassenarbeiten.

● Du kannst anhand dieser Übungen überprüfen, ob du alle vorangegangenen Übungen und Erklärungen richtig verstanden hast. Falls du die angegebene Endpunktzahl nicht erreichst, solltest du das Kapitel auf alle Fälle noch einmal durcharbeiten.

● Wenn du meinst, daß du ein Thema schon verstanden hast, kannst du diese Übungen auch sofort machen. So kannst du herausfinden, ob deine Einschätzung wirklich zutrifft. Falls du aber noch Fehler gemacht hast, solltest du unbedingt auch die Bleistiftübungen durcharbeiten.

♦ Die **puzzle pages** am Ende jedes Kapitels sind vor allem zur „Entspannung" gedacht. Auch hier werden Thema und Vokabeln des Kapitels noch einmal verarbeitet.

♦ Die **Lösungen** solltest du dir eigentlich erst ansehen, nachdem du die Übung selbständig durchgearbeitet hast. Wenn du aber Probleme hast, schau dir die Lösungen ruhig schon vorher an – es kann manchmal besser sein, so von „hinten nach vorn" zu arbeiten als einfach nur zu raten. Als „Mogelzettel" solltest du die Lösungen allerdings nicht benutzen – das hilft dir nicht.

Du solltest regelmäßig und gründlich mit dem Buch arbeiten. Das ist viel besser, als ein Kapitel übereilig und „in Panikstimmung" kurz vor einer Klassenarbeit durchzunehmen. Langsam Gelerntes sitzt sicher und fest!

Viel Spaß und Erfolg beim Arbeiten mit *Besser in Englisch*!

Die Autoren

WIR STELLEN UNS VOR!

DU TRIFFST UNS IN DIESEM BUCH..

I'M FREDDY CLARKE. HALLO! WE LIVE IN OAK LANE, TOO. THAT'S MUM, DAD, THE JAGUAR AND ME. THEY'RE ALWAYS CLEANING IT. WHAT I REALLY LIKE BEST ARE CAKES AND TOFFEES...
THIS IS OUR FORM TEACHER, MISS JOLLY. SHE'S OK.
...AND THIS IS OLD CARTER, THE MATHS TEACHER. HE'S DEFINITELY NOT OK ...
COLIN
TOM
JOHN
FREDDY
ELVIRA
MIKE
BOB
SALLY
JANE
MATHS IS FUN
MEANWHILE, AT THE COBB'S HOUSE..
SOME ANIMALS HAVE ALL THE FUN!
HALLO! I'M COCO. MY BOYFRIEND IS SPOOKY COBB. HERE WE ARE AT SPOOKY'S ... THE OTHERS HAVE GONE OUT...
WELL! I HOPE YOU ENJOYED MEETING EVERYONE ... I'M NESS, AND I'LL BE HELPING YOU WORK THROUGH THIS BOOK!
FOLLOW ME!

1

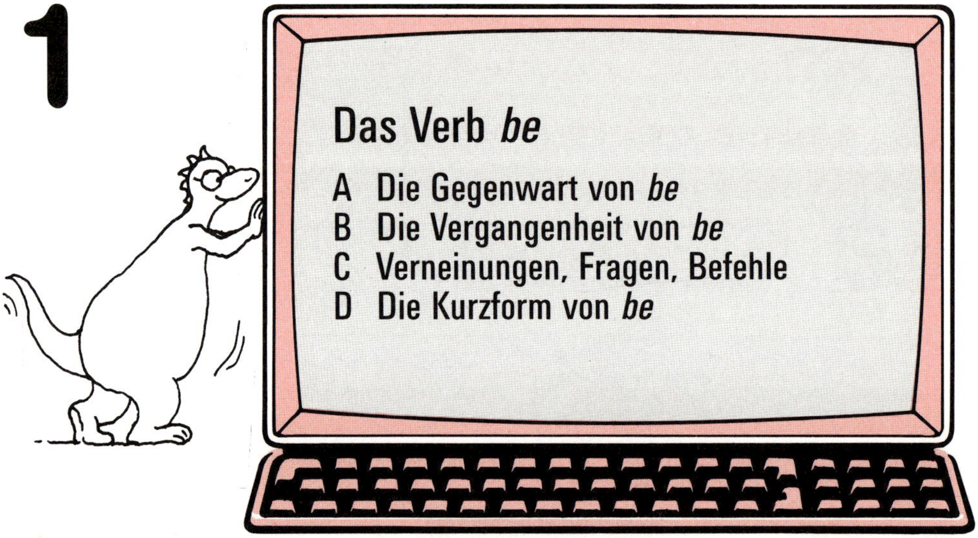

A Die Gegenwart von *be*

1 Bob Pratt: I **am** a pupil at Green Park School.
Sally Cobb: And I**'m** a pupil at Green Park, too.
2 Green Park School **is** in Kingston.
3 Bob**'s** captain of Green Park School football team.
4 They**'re** Bob's best friends.

- In den Sätzen oben steht das Verb *be* allein. Es ist also ein Vollverb.
- Wir bilden die Gegenwart von *be* wie folgt:

	bejaht		verneint	
	Langform	Kurzform	Langform	Kurzform
I	am	'm	am not	'm not
you	are	're	are not	're not/aren't
he	is	's	is not	's not/isn't
she	is	's	is not	's not/isn't
it	is	's	is not	's not/isn't
we	are	're	are not	're not/aren't
you	are	're	are not	're not/aren't
they	are	're	are not	're not/aren't

1 Setze die richtige Form von *be* ein. Benutze aber bitte nur die Langform.

My name is Bob Pratt. I ________ a pupil at Green Park School in Kingston. Kingston ________ a town near London. My best friends ________ Tom and Sally Cobb. They ________ pupils at Green Park, too. I ________ the captain of the Green Park football team, and Tom ________ the team goalkeeper. He ________ quite good, but I ________ the star. And Sally? She ________ great. She ________ also my girlfriend and head *(Leiter)* of my fan club.

B Die Vergangenheit von *be*

1 Tom: I **was** captain of the football team **last year.**
2 Sally **was** ill **yesterday,** but Tom **was** at school.
3 Tom and Sally **were** at Bob's party **last night.**

♦ Wir bilden die Vergangenheit von *be* wie folgt:

	bejaht	verneint	
		Langform	Kurzform
I	was	was not	wasn't
you	were	were not	weren't
he	was	was not	wasn't
she	was	was not	wasn't
it	was	was not	wasn't
we	were	were not	weren't
you	were	were not	weren't
they	were	were not	weren't

♦ Wir benutzen die Vergangenheit mit Signalwörtern wie *last year/ weekend/Saturday/summer/...; in 1985/...; yesterday.*

2 Setze die richtige Form der Vergangenheit von *be* ein.

1 Tom was ill last week, but Sally _____ at school.

2 In 1972 the Olympic Games _____ in Germany, and four years later they _____ in Canada.

3 – I _____ on holiday in Germany last summer, and it _____ wet *(naß)* and cold every day.

– Oh, it _____ bad everywhere last summer.

4 You _____ silly not to do your homework yesterday, Tom. Mr Carter _____ very angry with you, you know.

3 Setze die richtige Form der Gegenwart oder der Vergangenheit von *be* ein.

✔ = richtig; ✗ = falsch.

1 This school year, Miss Jolly _____ Tom's form teacher.

2 Miss Jolly: "Tom, _____ you ill yesterday afternoon? Mr Carter says you _____ not at his lesson again. You _____ quite OK in the lunch break yesterday."

3 Last year, Tom _____ the captain of the Green Park foot-ball team. He _____ quite good, but his friend Bob _____ the star. This year, Bob _____ the captain, but Tom and Bob _____ still good friends.

4 – Bob, where _____ your English book?

– I _____ sorry, Miss Jolly. I _____ late for the school bus this morning, and all my school things _____ at home.

– At home? They _____ no good at home, Bob.

– Yes, but I _____ here, Miss, and I _____ the star.

max. 16

Weniger als 12 Punkte? Wenn ja, arbeite bitte die Aufgaben 1, 2 und 3 nochmals durch!

C Verneinungen, Fragen, Befehle

1 **Is Tom** at Green Park School?
2 – **Were Bob and Sally** at the party last night?
– No, **they weren't** there. Sally was ill.
3 Miss Jolly: **Don't be** so silly, Tom. **Be quiet**, please.

♦ In verneinten Sätzen und Fragen funktioniert *be* genau wie „sein" im Deutschen 1 2.

♦ Bei der Befehlsform benutzt du einfach *be* bzw. *don't be* am Anfang des Satzes 3:

don't	*be*	Adjektiv	andere Satzteile
Don't	be	so silly,	Tom.
	Be	quiet,	please.

4 Die Sätze sind alle sachlich falsch.
Verneine sie und du bekommst richtige Aussagen heraus.

1 – London is in Scotland.
– No, that's wrong.
London _is not (isn't)_ in Scotland.

2 – Hamburgers are very good for you.
– Oh, no. They ________ at all good for you.

3 – The Rhine is the longest river in Europe.
– That's not right. The Rhine ________ the longest river in Europe.

4 – Hamsters are dangerous animals.
– That's silly. Hamsters ________ dangerous.

5 – Sally and Elvira were in Mr Wood's form last year.
– No, Sally and Elvira ________ in Mr Wood's form.

6 – Tom was captain of the football team last term *(Trimester)*.
– You're wrong. Tom ________ captain of the team.

7 – You are late again, Tom.
– No, Sir. I ________ late. It's only 10 o'clock.

5 Bitte bilde Fragen.

1 Sally is a good pupil.
Is Sally a good pupil?

2 Tom is often late for school.
______________________________?

3 Bob was captain last year.
______________________________?

4 Sally and Bob are good friends.
______________________________?

5 Tom and Sally were at Bob's party.
______________________________?

6 I am in the team for the next match.
______________________________?

6 Der arme Freddy Clarke macht scheinbar gar nichts richtig. Von allen Seiten bekommt er es zu hören!
Sage bitte Freddy Bescheid mit Sätzen mit *be/don't be*.

1 so noisy/quiet
Don't be so noisy, Freddy. Be quiet, please.

2 so lazy/helpful *(hilfsbereit)*
__________ so lazy, Freddy. __________, please.

3 so naughty/good
__________ so naughty, Freddy. __________, please.

4 so silly/sensible *(vernünftig)*
__________, Freddy. __________, please.

5 so careless/more careful
______________________________.

7 Bitte stelle Fragen, die diese Aussagen als Antwort hervorrufen könnten.

✔ = richtig; ✗ = falsch.

✔ 1 – Is Tom Cobb in Mr Wood's form?

– No, he's in Miss Jolly's form. (Tom Cobb)

2 – ______________________________ at King's School?

– No, they're at Green Park. (the Cobb children)

3 – ______________________________ a friendly teacher?

– No, but Miss Jolly is a friendly teacher. (Old Carter)

4 – ______________________________ the Clarkes' cat?

– Oh, no. He's the Cobbs' dog. (Spooky)

5 – ______________ next?

– No, I think Bob is next. (I)

6 – ______________________________ in France?

– No, they are in Germany. (Hamburg and Cologne)

7 – ______________________ captain of the team last year?

– No, Tom Cobb was captain last year. (Bob Pratt)

8 – ______________________________ expensive?

– No. They were quite cheap. (the bikes)

max. 7

Weniger als 4 Punkte? Wenn ja, arbeite bitte die Aufgaben 4 bis 7 nochmals durch!

D Die Kurzform von *be*

1 Tom**'s** a pupil at Green Park School, too.
2 I **am** not a very good dancer, but I**'m** quite a good singer.
3 Sally **wasn't** at school yesterday. She **was** ill.

♦ In Unterhaltungen und privaten Briefen/Postkarten benutzen wir die Kurzform.

♦ Hier sind weitere wichtige Kurzformen, die du dir merken mußt:

here's	= here is	**how's?**	= how is?
that's	= that is	**there's**	= there is
what's?	= what is?	**where's?**	= where is?
who's?	= who is?		

Du kannst die anderen Kurzformen von *be* in den Tabellen auf den Seiten 8 und 9 finden.

8 Unterstreiche die Kurzformen in dem Text.

It's Saturday, and Tom and Sally are waiting for their friends. They're having a party. "Where's the coke?" Sally said. "Tom, there's no coke." "Yes, there is," said Tom. "Twelve bottles. They're in the kitchen. That's enough, isn't it? I got it from Smith's. You know, the grocer's in Queen's Street. Coke's cheap there." "Oh," Sally said, "you're just like dad. He's always looking at how much things cost, too." "What's wrong with that?" Tom said. "We're not rich, are we?"

9 Die Unterhaltung unten klingt sehr unnatürlich, weil nur die Langform benutzt wird.
Benutze die Kurzform, um den Dialog lockerer und freundlicher zu machen.

✔ = richtig; ✗ = falsch.

✔ *Tom* (Miss Jolly is) Miss Jolly's nice, but (Mr Carter is not) ________ so good. (He is) ________ very strict *(streng)*. I am glad when Maths is over.

Sally Oh, come on, Tom. (Old Carter is) ________ OK. (You are) ________ lazy, (that is) ________ all. (You are) ________ often late for his lessons, and (you are) ________ cheeky *(frech)* to him, too. (I am) ________ not surprised *(überrascht)* that (he is) ________ sometimes angry with you.

Bob Yes, (Sally is) ________ right, Tom. Last week (you were not) ________ at the Maths lesson on Wednesday afternoon. And (you were not) ________ ill.

max. 12

Weniger als 9 Punkte? Wenn ja, arbeite bitte die Aufgaben 8 und 9 nochmals durch!

1 Das Verb *be* · Seite 16

Quiz

Finde die richtige Antwort. Hast du alle acht richtig benannt, so ergeben die Buchstaben hinter den richtigen Antworten eine Stadt in Schottland.

1 Who is Rod Stewart?
- a racing driver (G)
- a teacher at your school (E)
- a pop star (A)

2 What is the capital of Scotland?
- Edinburgh (B)
- Glasgow (R)
- London (S)

3 Where was Julius Caesar born?

- Britain (L)
- Italy (E)
- Germany (B)

4 What are dandelions?
- African animals (H)
- flowers (R)
- chocolates (O)

5 Where is Piccadilly Circus?
- New York (T)
- London (D)
- Sydney (M)

6 Where is Dublin?
- Wales (C)
- Holland (S)
- Ireland (E)

7 Who has been the British Queen since 1952?
- Diana (F)
- Elizabeth II (E)
- Beatrix (U)

8 Who were the Beatles?
- pop singers (N)
- footballers (I)
- teachers (D)

The town is ____.

2

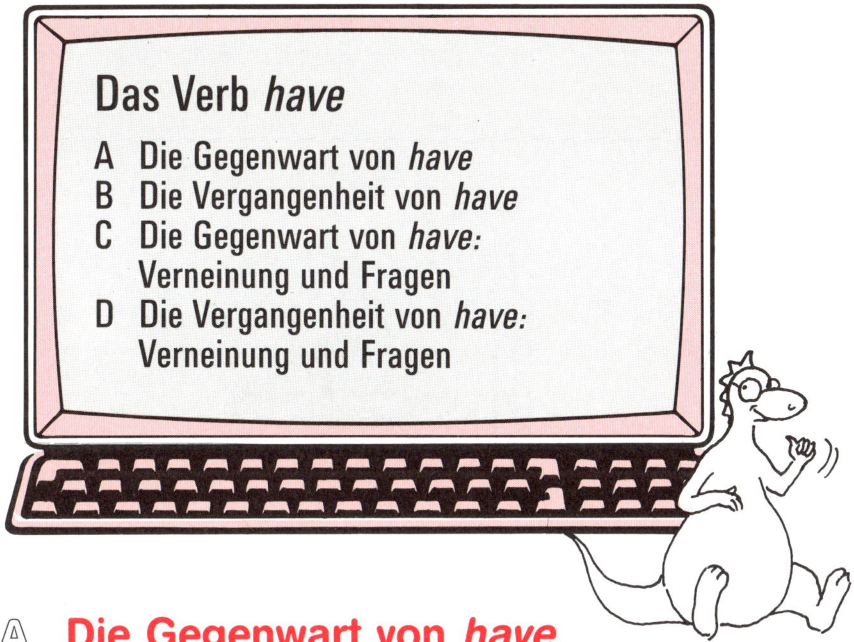

A Die Gegenwart von *have*

1 Bob **has got** a new football.
2 I always **have** breakfast before I go to school.
3 We **have** a great holiday every summer.

♦ Wir bilden die Gegenwart von *have* wie folgt:

	bejaht		verneint	
	Langform	Kurzform	Langform	Kurzform
I	have	I've	have not	haven't
you	have	you've	have not	haven't
he	has	–	has not	hasn't
she	has	–	has not	hasn't
it	has	–	has not	hasn't
we	have	we've	have not	haven't
you	have	you've	have not	haven't
they	have	they've	have not	haven't

♦ Wenn *have* „besitzen" bedeutet, benutzen wir das Wörtchen *got*, um diese Verwendung von *have* zu verstärken:

- Bob **has got** a new football.
  Bob hat/besitzt einen neuen Fußball.

1 Setze die Langform der Gegenwart von *have* ein. Benutze *got*, wenn *have* eindeutig „besitzen" bedeutet.

1 Sally and Tom have got a little dog called Spooky. Spooky __________ a lovely face and always has milk for breakfast. Spooky likes it when Sally __________ time for him after school. Then he __________ his walk in Green Park and __________ a lot of fun with the other dogs there.

2 *Mr Carter* Tom Cobb, I can see that you __________ something under the desk.

Tom I __________________ my pencil, Sir, that's all.

Mr Carter No, no, Cobb. You __________________ a toy. Give it to me, boy! I ______________ some nice little Maths exercises for you after school.

3 – Great. Tom always __________ a super party on his birthday. We all __________ a great time. Tom always __________ lots of cakes, coke and ice-cream.

– Not this time. Poor Tom says he ____________ no money. He __________ only bread and mineral water for us.

B Die Vergangenheit von *have*

1 I **had** a great holiday in France last summer.
2 We **had** a wonderful time at Tom's party yesterday.
3 Sally **had got** her Maths book, so she gave it to Tom.

♦ Wir bilden die Vergangenheit von *have* wie folgt:

	bejaht	verneint	
		Langform	Kurzform
I	had	had not	hadn't
you	had	had not	hadn't
he	had	had not	hadn't
she	had	had not	hadn't
it	had	had not	hadn't
we	had	had not	hadn't
you	had	had not	hadn't
they	had	had not	hadn't

♦ Auch in der Vergangenheit benutzen wir das Wörtchen *got*, um die besitzanzeigende Bedeutung von *have* klar zu zeigen 3.

2 Setze die Vergangenheit von *have* ein.
Benutze das Stützwort *got*, wo ein Sternchen (*) steht.

1 Yesterday, Sally _had_ a bad cold *(Erkältung)*, so she ________ a day in bed.

2 I ________ a great time at the Wild Cats disco last night. Bob Pratt was there, and we ________ a lot of fun together.

3 – Tom and Bob ________ a bad fight in the playground today.
– Oh? Why?
– Because Bob said Tom ________* his new football.
– And?
– Well, Bob was right. Tom ________* his silly football, but what's a football between friends *(unter Freunden)*?

3 Setze die Gegenwart oder die Vergangenheit von *have* ein. Benutze *got* nur dann, wenn *have* eindeutig „besitzen" bedeutet.

✔ = richtig; ✗ = falsch.

1 – Oh no! I __________ no football things again.

– Ask Tom. He __________ his things with him, and he can't play today. He __________ extra Maths to do for Mr Carter.

2 We __________ a great time last Sunday. We went and __________ a super Chinese meal at the Ho-Ho-Ho. We all __________ so much to eat that we went home and __________ a good sleep in the afternoon.

3 – We __________ rain on Monday, we __________ rain yesterday and we __________ more rain today. I'm so bored!

– Don't be silly, Tom. You __________ books, records, games. You __________ so many interesting things to do. And what about homework? You __________ Maths at school today, so I'm sure you __________ some homework from Mr Carter. You always __________ lots of homework from him.

max. 15

Weniger als 12 Punkte? Wenn ja, arbeite bitte die Aufgaben 1 bis 3 nochmals durch!

Ⓒ Die Gegenwart von *have*: Verneinung und Fragen

1. I **haven't got** a dog.
2. We **don't have** Maths on Tuesdays.
3. **Have** the Cobbs **got** a dog or a cat?
4. **Do** you **have** just coffee for breakfast?
5. **Does** Freddy **have** a holiday in France every summer?

♦ Bei *have got* bilden wir verneinte Sätze und Fragen ohne das Hilfsverb *do* 1 3.

♦ Sonst bilden wir verneinte Sätze und Fragen mit *do/does*, genau wie bei anderen Vollverben 2 4 5.

4 Bilde Fragen und verneinte Sätze, wie in den Beispielsätzen unten angegeben.

- ● Sally has got a new coat.
- ▶ Has Sally got a new coat?
- ▶ Sally has not got (hasn't got) a new coat.

- ● Sally has tea in the afternoon.
- ▶ Does Sally have tea in the afternoon?
- ▶ Sally does not (doesn't) have tea in the afternoon.

1 Tom Cobb has got a new bike.

______________________ a new bike?

Tom Cobb ______________________ a new bike.

2 Tom and Sally have got lots of nice books.

______________________ lots of nice books?

Tom and Sally ______________________ lots of nice books.

3 Elvira has some milk for breakfast.

______________________ some milk for breakfast?

Elvira ______________________ for breakfast.

4 Bob and Tom have a good time at the youth club every week.

______________________ at the youth club every week?

Bob and Tom ______________________

______________________.

5 We have a Chinese meal on Saturdays.

______________________ a Chinese meal on Saturdays?

We ______________________ a Chinese meal on Saturdays.

6 I have got some felt-tip pens.

_______ you ______________________?

______________________.

Ⓓ Die Vergangenheit von *have*: Verneinung und Fragen

1 We **didn't have** much fun at Bob's party.
2 **Did** you **have** something to eat before you came to school?

♦ In der Vergangenheit bilden wir verneinte Sätze und Fragen mit *did*, genau wie bei anderen Vollverben.

5 Bilde verneinte Sätze und Fragen, wie in den Beispielsätzen unten angegeben.

- Tom had got his books yesterday.
- ▸ Tom did not (didn't) have his books yesterday.
- ▸ Did Tom have his books yesterday?

1 Elvira had extra homework yesterday.

____________________ extra homework yesterday.

____________________ extra homework yesterday?

2 Sally and Tom had bikes for Christmas.

____________________ bikes for Christmas.

____________________ bikes for Christmas?

3 Bob had a quarrel *(Streit)* with Elvira today.

____________________ a quarrel with Elvira today.

____________________ a quarrel with Elvira today?

4 Professor Hudd had an accident on his way home.

____________________ on his way home.

____________________ on his way home?

5 I had a good time at the weekend.

____

____?

6 Sieh dir die Bilder an, und schreibe dazu verneinte Sätze bzw. Fragen, wie in den Beispielsätzen vorgegeben.

✔ = richtig; ✗ = falsch.

✔ 1 Has Tom got a moped? (Tom)

✔ 2 Miss Jolly didn't have a nice holiday last year. (Miss Jolly)

3 ______________________________ telephones. (The Romans)

4 ______________________________ a car? (Mr and Mrs Cobb)

5 ______________________________ a dog. (Bob)

6 ______________________________

________ hamburgers? (Robin Hood)

7 ______________________________

_____________ a house? (Mr Carter)

8 ______________________________

_____ supermarkets. (the old Greeks)

9 ______________________________

______________ a colour TV. (Elvira)

10 __________ you __________

________________ a nice weekend?

max. **8**

Weniger als 5 Punkte? Wenn ja, arbeite bitte die Aufgaben 4 bis 6 nochmals durch!

Der Zauberbaum

Farmer Jones ist sehr glücklich. Er hat einen Baum, der alle Früchte und Gemüsesorten trägt.
Sieh dir Farmer Jones herrlichen Zauberbaum an, und schreibe unten – in Englisch – auf, welche verschiedenen Obst- und Gemüsearten – und wie viele davon – du gefunden hast.

Farmer Jones has got three apples, ______ o______, ______ s______, ______ b______, ______ p______, ______ t______, ______ cabbage and ______ carrots on his magic tree.

3

A *Do* als Vollverb

1 I always **do** my homework before I go to bed. *(erledigen)*
2 Sally always **does** her best at school. *(tun, machen)*
3 Elvira **did** the shopping yesterday. *(erledigen)*

♦ Das Verb *do* hat folgende Formen:

Gegenwart:	do/does	do not (don't)/does not (doesn't)
Vergangenheit:	did	did not (didn't)

1 Setze die richtige Form von *do* in die Sätze ein.

1 Bob often ________________ the shopping for his mother.
2 Freddy ________________ his homework in the bus yesterday.
3 When Mrs Cobb is ill, the children __________ the housework.
4 At school, Elvira ______________ well in painting and dancing.
5 Bob and Tom ___________ some football training last Monday.
6 Miss Jolly ______________________ her driving test last week.
7 In Britain, small children _________ their homework at school.
8 Sally ________________ breakfast for her parents on Sundays.

B *Do* als Hilfsverb: Fragen

do	Subjekt	Vollverb	andere Teile	Kurzantwort
Do	they	go	to Green Park School?	Yes, they do.
Does	Bob	live	in Oak Lane, too?	Yes, he does.
Did	Sally	go	to Elvira's party?	No, she didn't.

♦ Bei Fragen erscheint das *-s* für die 3. Person Singular nicht mehr beim Vollverb, sondern nur beim Hilfsverb *does*.

Aussage: Bob lives in Oak Lane, too.

Frage: Does Bob live in Oak Lane, too?

♦ Fragen im Imperfekt werden mit *did* eingeleitet, und das Vollverb steht dann in dem Infinitiv.

Aussage: Sally **went** to Elvira's party.
Frage: **Did** Sally **go** to Elvira's party?

2 Bilde Fragen mit *do/does/did* und schreibe die entsprechende Kurzantwort dazu.

1 Bob thinks he is the great star. (Yes)
Does Bob think he is the great star?
Yes, he does.

2 Tom laughed at Mr Carter today. (No)
Did Tom laugh at Mr Carter today?
No, he didn't.

3 The children live in Oak Lane. (Yes)
______________________ in Oak Lane?
Yes, they __________.

4 Spooky went to the vet's *(Tierarzt)* yesterday. (No)
______________________ to the vet's yesterday?
No, he __________.

5 Green Park won the match. (No)

______________________________ the match?

No, they ______________.

6 Freddy eats too many toffees. (Yes)

______________________________ too many toffees?

______________________.

7 Mr Carter got angry with Tom today. (No)

______________________________ with Tom today?

______________________.

8 Elvira helps her mother a lot. (Yes)

______________________________________.

______________________.

9 Tom and Sally bought some new jeans on Saturday. (No)

______________________________________.

______________________.

Ⓒ *Do* als Hilfsverb: die Verneinung

	Subjekt	*do*	*not*	Vollverb	andere Satzteile
1	They	**do**	**not**	go	to King's School.
2	He	**does**	**not**	play	handball.
3	She	**did**	**not**	watch	videos.

♦ Genau wie bei der Fragebildung ändert sich nur das Hilfsverb *do*, um die Zeiten, also Gegenwart und Vergangenheit, anzuzeigen. Auch hier ist es sehr wichtig, sich zu merken, daß das Vollverb immer im Infinitiv steht.

3 Die Sätze unten sind alle sachlich falsch.
Stelle sie richtig mit Hilfe der Angaben.

1 Bob plays basketball. (football)

Bob does not play basketball. He plays football.

2 Mr Cobb works in London. (Kingston)

He ____________________ in London.

He ________________ in Kingston.

3 Mrs Nunn likes gardening. (cooking)

She ________________ gardening. She ___________ cooking.

4 Bob and Tom live in Ash St. (Oak Lane)

Bob and Tom _______________ in Ash St. They __________ in Oak Lane.

5 Freddy eats a lot of fruit. (toffees)

He ____________ much fruit. He ___________ a lot of toffees.

6 Miss Jolly goes out with Mr Taylor. (Mr Carter)

She ____

____

7 The children watch videos at the weekend. (play games/read)

They ____

____

4 Übersetze die unterstrichenen Teile der folgenden Sätze ins Englische.

✔ = richtig; ✗ = falsch.

1 Wohnt Elvira auch in der Oak Lane?

____

2 Samstags gehen britische Kinder nicht in die Schule.

____

3 Gestern gingen wir nicht ins Kino.

____

4 Spielen Tom und Bob Fußball oder Handball?

____

5 Helfen die Kinder auch im Garten?

____

6 Liest du gern Bücher?

____

max. 6

Weniger als 4 Punkte? Wenn ja, arbeite bitte die Aufgaben 1 bis 4 nochmals durch!

D *Do* als Hilfsverb: die verneinte Befehlsform

1 **Don't be** so silly, Tom.
2 **Don't make** such a noise, children.

♦ Die verneinte Befehlsform wird mit *do not/don't* + Infinitiv des Vollverbs gebildet, und zwar im Singular und auch im Plural.

5 Die Schilder unten sind alle Verbotsschilder.
Bilde Sätze mit *don't*, um jemandem zu sagen, was die Schilder bedeuten.

1 (cross) Don't cross the road.

2 (feed) ____________ ____________ the animals.

3 (swim) ____________ ____________ in the river.

4 (throw) ____________ out of the window.

5 (smoke) ____________ ____________ in the train.

6 (play) ____________ ____________ radios on the beach.

7 (play) ____________ ____________ in the car park.

8 (pick) ____________ ____________.

E *Do* als Vollverb und Hilfsverb

	Hilfsverb	Subjekt	Hilfsverb	Vollverb	andere Satzteile
1		I	**don't**	**do**	the shopping.
2	**Does**	Sally		**do**	her brother's bed?
3	**Did**	you		**do**	the cooking ...?

♦ Laß dich nicht verwirren. In diesen Sätzen tritt *do* nämlich zweifach auf, und zwar als Vollverb und als Hilfsverb.

♦ Wie die Aufstellung zeigt, bleibt das Vollverb *do* im Infinitiv. Nur das Hilfsverb *do* ändert sich je nach Person und Zeit.

6 In dieser Übung sollst du die Fragen stellen. Schreibe die entsprechende Kurzantwort dazu.

1 Sally does the beds every day.

Does Sally do the beds every day? No, *she doesn't.*

2 Tom does the housework sometimes.

____________________ the housework sometimes?

Yes, ____________________.

3 The Cobbs do the garden on Saturdays.

____________________ the garden on Saturdays?

Yes, ____________________.

4 Bob and Tom do their rooms every day.

____________________ their rooms every day?

No, ____________________.

5 Freddy did the washing-up last night.

____?

No, ____________________.

6 Tom and Sally do their English together.

____?

Yes, ____________________.

7 Benutze die Satzteile, um Sätze mit *do* zu bilden.

✔ = richtig; ✗ = falsch.

1 (Mrs Nunn/the housework)

✔ Mrs Nunn does the housework in the evenings.

2 (Mr Cobb/the gardening)

Did Mr Cobb ______________________ yesterday?

3 (Bob/his homework)

______________________ every afternoon?

4 (Tom and Sally/not/the shopping)

____

______________________ last Saturday.

5 (Miss Jolly/her hair)

______________________ every day.

6 (Elvira/not/her bed)

______________________ every morning .

7 (The boys and girls/a Maths test)

____

______________________ last Friday?

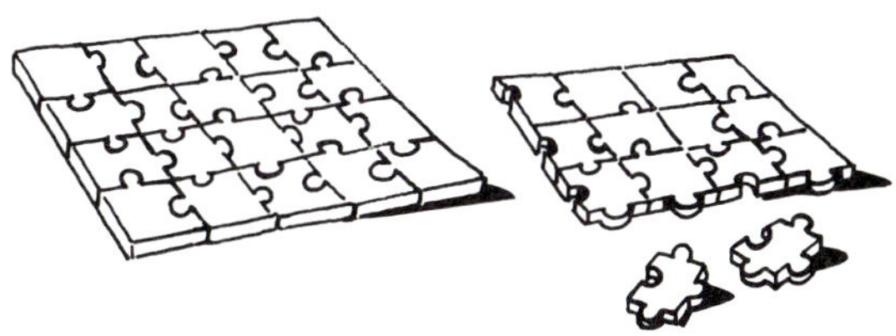

8 (We/two jigsaw puzzles)

______________________ yesterday.

9 (Freddy/not/the washing-up)

____

______________________ at the weekends.

max. 8

Weniger als 6 Punkte? Wenn ja, arbeite bitte die Aufgaben 5 bis 7 nochmals durch!

Do you come from Dover?

Sieh dir die Bilder an. Überlege, wie die dargestellten Personen, Tiere bzw. Gegenstände im Englischen heißen. Trage die Wörter in die entsprechende Lücke ein, aber in alphabetischer Reihenfolge.

Do ____________________

Do ____________________

Do ____________________

Do ____________________

Do ____________________

Do ____________________

Do ____________________

Do ____________________

4

A How? what? when? where? who? why?

1 **How do you make** a milk pudding?
2 **What are you doing** at the weekend, Tom?
3 **When can Bob come round** today?
4 **Who can I ask** to my party?

♦ Bei Fragen, die mit *how?, when?,* usw. gebildet sind, stellen wir das Fragewort einfach an den Anfang des Fragesatzes.

Frage ohne Fragewort:	Can Bob come round today?
Frage mit Fragewort:	**When** can Bob come round today?

1 Benutze die unterstrichenen Satzteile, um Fragen mit *how?, what?, when?, where?, who?, why?* zu bilden.

1 Tom and Sally Cobb live in Oak Lane, Kingston.
Where do Tom and Sally Cobb live?

2 Tom and Bob played football yesterday.
What did Tom and Bob do yesterday afternoon?

3 Elvira gets up at 7 every morning.

____

4 I am late because I missed the bus, Miss.

you

5 Sally gives Tweets water every morning.

6 I saw Elvira at the youth club disco yesterday.

you

7 The post office is in Briany Road next to the pub.

8 Look, Sally, you switch on the cooker like this.

B *What?* und *who?* als Subjekt

	Objekt	Hilfsverb	Subjekt	Vollverb	andere Satzteile
1	**What**	are	you	doing	in the garden, Freddy?
2	**Who**	do	you	like	best, Bob or Tom?
3			**What**	happened	to your bike, Tom?
4			**Who**	is coming	to your party, Elvira?

♦ In den Sätzen 1 und 2 sind *what?* und *who?* Objekt des Satzes. Wir brauchen immer ein Hilfsverb, also *do, are* usw., um die Frage zu bilden.

♦ In den Sätzen 3 und 4 sind *what?* und *who?* Subjekt des Satzes. In diesem Fall brauchen wir kein Hilfsverb, um eine Frage zu bilden.

2 Bilde Fragen mit *what?, who?*.
In dieser Übung bildet das Fragewort immer das Subjekt des Satzes.

1 – Who goes out with Bob every weekend? – Sally does.

2 – ____________ is making that noise? – Spooky is.

3 – ____________ often sings a lovely song? – Tweets does.

4 – ________ happened at school yesterday? – A bad accident.

5 – ______________ likes playing with Coco? – Spooky does.

6 – ______________________ hit poor Mr Carter on the head?

– Tom's football did.

3 Benutze die unterstrichenen Satzteile, um Fragen mit *how? what? when? where? who? why?* zu bilden.
In Sätzen mit *who?* oder *what?* achte besonders darauf, ob es sich um das Subjekt oder das Objekt des Satzes handelt.

✔ = richtig; ✗ = falsch.

1 We are having fish and chips for tea today.

✔ What are we having for tea today?

2 Miss Jolly is angry because Tom missed Maths again.

____

3 An accident happened at work today.

____

4 I stayed at home and read a book yesterday.

____________________ you ____________________

5 Sally danced with Tom at Elvira's party.

____

6 Elvira loves Bob Pratt.

____

7 We have lunch at 12 o'clock.

____________________ you ____________________

8 You do that sum *(Rechenaufgabe)* like this.

____

9 Elvira Nunn lives in Apple Road.

____

max. 8

Weniger als 6 Punkte? Wenn ja, arbeite bitte die Aufgaben 1 bis 3 nochmals durch!

C Whose?

1	– **Whose** book is this? – (It's) Elvira's.
2	– **Whose** records are these? – (They're) Sally's.

♦ Wir benutzen *whose?*, um zu fragen, wem irgend etwas gehört.

4 Sieh dir die Bilder an, und stelle Fragen mit *whose?*

1

Whose dog is Spooky?

(dog)

2

____

____

__________ Tweets? (bird)

3

____

____

_____ Miss Jolly? (form teacher)

4

____

____

________ Freddy? (neighbour)

Mixed-up questions and answers

Die Fragen und Antworten sind durcheinander gekommen. Verbinde die Fragen mit den Antworten, indem du den Antworten die Nummern der entsprechenden Fragen zuordnest.

Questions

1 Hello, what's your name?
2 Where do you live?
3 Who is your teacher?
4 How old are you?
5 Are you British?
6 What are your hobbies?
7 Can you speak German?
8 When is your birthday?
9 Where are you going on holiday?
10 Have you ever been to Germany?
11 What is your worst subject at school?

Answers

( ) Yes, I am.
( ) Bournemouth.
( ) In London.
( ) No, I haven't been there yet, but I'd like to go.
( ) History.
( ) 13.
( ) May 13th.
( ) Miss Gardner.
( ) Well, just a little.
(1) Sarah Black.
( ) Dancing, swimming and going to the cinema.

5

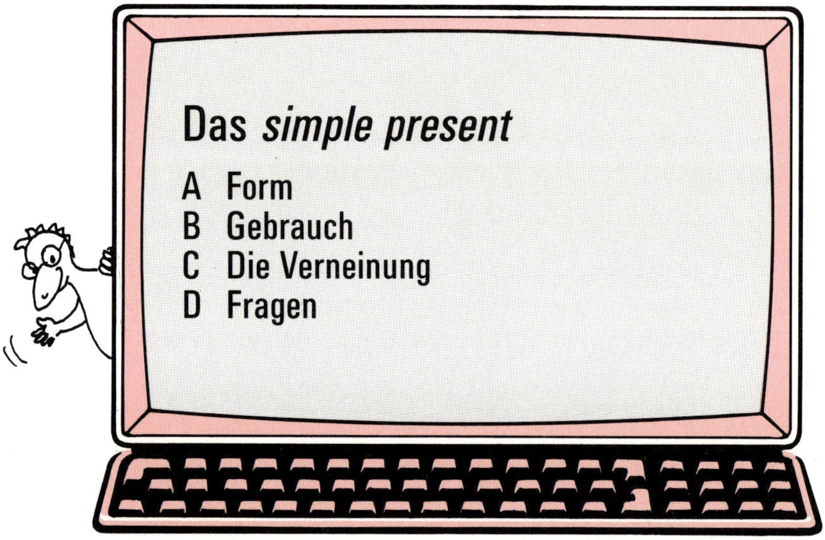

A Form

1 Every year Sally's friends **come** to her birthday party.
2 Elvira sometimes **brings** a cake.
3 Bob often **dances** with Sally at her party.
4 Tom and Freddy always **play** cards at parties.

♦ Wir bilden das *simple present* wie folgt:

	simple present	
I	play	go
you	play	go
he	play**s**	go**es**
she	play**s**	go**es**
it	play**s**	go**es**
we	play	go
you	play	go
they	play	go

♦ Ganz so einfach ist es mit dem Anhängen von *-s* nicht.
Es gibt bestimmte Schreibregeln, die du beachten mußt:

- Bei einem Zischlaut *(-sh, -ss, -ch, -x)* benutzen wir *-es:*

wash	▸ he wash**es**	watch	▸ he watch**es**
kiss	▸ she kiss**es**	mix	▸ it mix**es**

- Das *-y* nach einem Konsonanten wird zum *-i*. Hinzu kommt *-es:*
  try ▸ he tr**ies**
  cry ▸ she cr**ies**
- Das *-y* nach einem Vokal bleibt. Hinzu kommt nur *-s:*
  say ▸ he say**s**

1 Unterstreiche alle Verben, die im *simple present* stehen.

The Cobbs live in England. They have two children. The children go to school by bus every morning. Mr Cobb works in Kingston. He always drives to work. He often needs an hour. At the weekend the children often play cricket with their friends and their dog, Spooky. They sometimes go for a picnic. Their friends often come from Germany and stay for two weeks. They always bring salami and marzipan with them. Mrs Cobb likes German salami very much.

2 Schreibe die Form der folgenden Verben im *simple present* auf.

like/he he likes	push/he ______
cry/she ______	swim/she ______
cut/it ______	teach/they ______
dress/she ______	wash/I ______
find/he ______	eat/she ______
fly/it ______	go/he ______

B Gebrauch

1 In Germany, people **speak** German.
2 He sometimes **brings** a cake.
3 He often **dances** with her.

♦ Wir benutzen das *simple present,* um etwas auszudrücken, was immer so ist 1 und, um zu sagen, was man manchmal, oft, immer usw. macht 2 3.

♦ Deshalb treten folgende Zeitadverbien sehr häufig mit dem *simple present* zusammen auf. Sie alle drücken eine Regelmäßigkeit aus und gelten deshalb als Signalwörter für das *simple present:*

- always, never
- often, sometimes, now and then
- usually, normally, regularly
- every day, every week, every ...
- on Mondays/..., at weekends/Christmas/...

3 Suche für jeden Satz ein passendes Verb von der Liste aus.
Du mußt die Verben aber – je nach Person – ändern und auch die Rechtschreibung beachten.

catch – eat – finish – get up – go – make – read – ring up – talk – wash – watch – work – write

Every Monday it's the same story. Bob __________ at 7 o'clock. He __________ breakfast. Then he __________ the bus to school. His dad __________ in the same *(gleiche)* part of town. But he __________ by bike. Bob's mother __________ the clothes and __________ the dinner. She __________ her work at 2 o'clock. Sometimes she __________ her friends and __________ for hours! In the evening Bob __________ TV and his dad __________ his newspaper. His mother __________ letters to her friends.

4 Benutze die Tabelle unten, um acht vollständige Sätze über die Aktivitäten von Bob, Sally und Elvira zu schreiben.

✔ = richtig; ✗ = falsch.

	Bob	Sally and Elvira
every morning	get up at 7 o'clock	make breakfast
always	come home from school at 4 o'clock	go to school by bus
on Saturdays	buy a comic	play basketball
often	listen to records	meet their friends
never	walk to school	do the cooking

✔ 1 Bob gets up at 7 o'clock every morning.

2 He ____________________

3 He ____________________

4 He ____________________

5 He ____________________

✔ 6 Sally and Elvira make breakfast every morning.

7 They ____________________

8 They ____________________

9 They ____________________

10 They ____________________

max. **8**

Weniger als 6 Punkte? Wenn ja, arbeite bitte die Aufgaben 1 bis 4 nochmals durch!

Ⓒ Die Verneinung

1	Elvira **can't** speak German.
2	We **don't like** hamburgers and chips much.
3	Freddy loves toffees, but **doesn't like** marzipan.

♦ Wenn es schon ein Hilfsverb im Satz gibt, brauchen wir nur das Wörtchen *not/n't* unmittelbar dahinter zu setzen 1.

♦ Wenn aber kein Hilfsverb vorhanden ist, müssen wir das Hilfsverb *do* um Hilfe bitten 2 3.

5 Ergänze die Sätze mit Hilfe der Bilder.

1 Tom plays football but he

doesn't play hockey.

2 A baker sells bread but he

____

3 My cat drinks milk but she

____

4 The boys run home but they

____

5 I speak English but

____

6 Jim loves Janet but Janet

____

7 Cats sleep during the day but

____

8 My mother makes bread but

____

D Fragen

Hilfsverb	Subjekt	Adverb	Vollverb	Objekt	andere Satzteile
1 **Can**	you		swim?		
2 **Must**	we		go		to school on Saturday?
3 **Do**	you	often	watch	TV?	
4 **Does**	Spooky	always	bark		at the postman?

♦ Wenn kein anderes Hilfsverb, z. B. *can* oder *must,* zur Verfügung steht, müssen wir *do/does* benutzen, um die Frageform zu bilden.

6 Benutze die Aussagesätze unten, um Fragen zu bilden.

1 Spooky likes cats.

Does Spooky like cats?

2 Mr Carter comes from Liverpool.

____________________ from Liverpool?

3 We live in a big house.

_____ you _______________ in a big house?

4 The boys always run across the road.

____________________ across the road?

5 Elvira has got a new pair of dancing shoes.

_______________ a new pair of dancing shoes?

6 The Queen can go on holiday four times a year.

_______________ on holiday four times a year?

7 Bob often writes a postcard to his friend in Canada.

____________________ to his friend in Canada?

7 Bilde Sätze mit den Satzteilen. Beachte dabei die Symbole am Anfang der Schreiblinien:

[+] = Aussagesatz, [–] = verneinter Satz, und [?] = Fragesatz.

✔ = richtig; ✗ = falsch.

1 Freddy/always/tease *(ärgern)*/Tweets

✔ [+] Freddy always teases Tweets.

2 my father/work/in London

[+] ______________________

3 he/never/listen/to pop records

[–] ______________________

4 fish/live/in water

[?] ______________________

5 Dirk's sister/sometimes/help/him with his homework

[?] ______________________

____

6 Colin/often/write/to his grandmother/in Canada

[+] ______________________

____

7 we/watch/a lot of TV/at the weekend

[–] ______________________

____

8 the supermarket/sell/English books

[–] ______________________

____

9 dogs/sleep/at night

[?] ______________________

max. 8

Weniger als 6 Punkte? Wenn ja, arbeite bitte die Aufgaben 5 bis 7 nochmals durch!

Where are the verbs?

Irgend jemand hat sich einen Scherz erlaubt. Er hat die Verben aus der Geschichte herausgeschnitten.
Du kannst aber das jeweils richtige Verb leicht wiederfinden. Du brauchst nur die Form der Lücke mit der Form des herausgeschnittenen Verbs zu vergleichen!

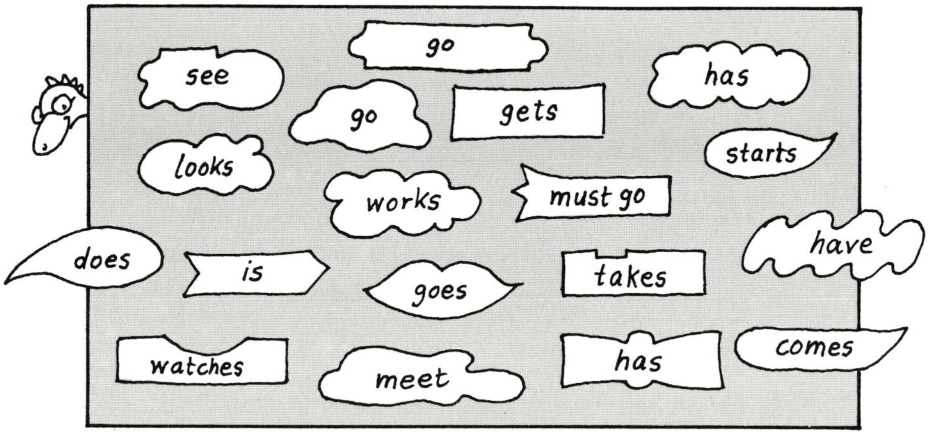

The children ______ 1 to school every morning. They sometimes ______ 2 Spooky in the road. He often ______ 3 a newspaper but sometimes he ______ 4 a bone from the butcher. He always ______ 5 happy. Mrs Cobb ______ 6 at home. Mr Cobb ______ 7 to the office. He 8 ______ work at 9 o'clock. He ______ 9 never later. Sometimes he ______ 10 the car but usually he ______ 11 by bus. He 12 ______ home at 6 o'clock and ______ 13 TV after tea. Sally and Tom often 14 ______ their friends after school. They sometimes ______ 15 to a snack-bar where they often ______ 16 a lemonade. Tom always ______ 17 to wash the car on Saturdays and Sally 18 ______ the shopping for her mother.

6

Das *present progressive*

A Form
B Gebrauch
C Die Verneinung
D Fragen
E Das *simple present* und das *present progressive* im Vergleich

A Form

1 – Sally, where's Spooky?
– Don't worry. He **is playing** in the garden.
2 Quick! The bus **is stopping.** We get out here.
3 – Where are you, Elvira?
– In my bedroom. I'**m making** my bed and putting my jeans away.

◆ Wir bilden das *present progressive* wie folgt:

	bejaht	verneint
	Langform/Kurzform	Langform/Kurzform
I	am/'m playing	am not/'m not playing
you	are/'re playing	are not/'re not playing
he/she/it	is/'s playing	is not/'s not/isn't playing
we/you/they	are/'re playing	are/'re not playing

◆ Wenn wir das *present progressive* schreiben, müssen wir die folgenden Schreibregeln beachten:

- bei Verben, die auf *-e* enden, lassen wir bei der Bildung der *-ing*-Form den Endbuchstaben *-e* weg:
  ma**ke** ▸ making
- bei Verben, die mit einem kurzen Vokal + folgenden Konsonant, wie *-m, -n, -p,* oder *-t* enden, wird der Konsonant verdoppelt:
  sto**p** ▸ sto**pp**ing   pu**t** ▸ pu**tt**ing

1 Hier sollst du die vollständige Form des *present progressive* der angegebenen Verben in die Sätze einsetzen.

1 Tom <u>is doing</u> (do) his homework at the moment, and Sally ____________ (help) her dad in the garden. They ____________ (cut) the grass.

2 Tom and Sally ____________ (tidy up) their rooms. Tom ____________ (put) his clothes and books away, and Sally ____________ (make) her bed.

3 – Elvira, where are you?
– I ____________ (watch) TV, Mum.

4 Hallo, Fans! I ____________ (have) a great time on holiday in Bournemouth. I ____________ (write) this on the beach. Sally ____________ (swim) in the sea, and of course Spooky ____________ (run) up and down. He ____________ (bark) at her. And my parents? They ____________ (sleep), as usual.

B Gebrauch

1	Tom and Sally **are helping** their father **at the moment.**
2	I can't help you **now,** Tom. I**'m washing** my hair.
3	Look! What **is** Spooky **doing**?

♦ Wir benutzen das *present progressive,* um eine Handlung zu beschreiben, die zur Zeit des Sprechens oder Schreibens gerade geschieht, also im Gange ist.

♦ Im Deutschen kennen wir die Verlaufsform des Verbs nicht. Wir benutzen die Adverbien „im Moment", „jetzt" oder „gerade".

- Ich kann nicht kommen. Ich **wasche** mir **gerade** die Haare.
  I can't come. I**'m washing** my hair.

♦ Das *present progressive* wird häufig mit den Signalwörtern *now, at the moment* und *at present* benutzt.

2 Sieh dir die Bilder an, und sage, was Sally, Tom usw. gerade machen.

1 Bob is scoring a goal.

(score/a goal)

2 ______________________

____

(sing/in her cage)

3 ______________________

____

(run/to the bus-stop)

4 ______________________

____

(practise/a new dance)

5 ______________________

____

(make/a bed)

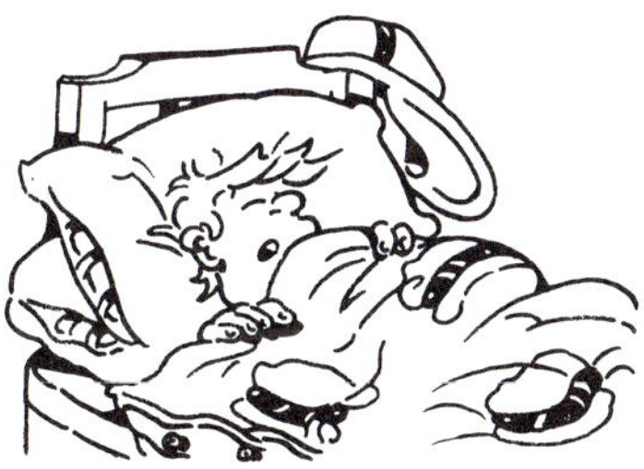

6 ______________________

____

(sleep/in bed)

3 Übersetze die Sätze ins Englische.

✔ = richtig; ✗ = falsch.

1 Ich spiele gerade mit meinem kleinen Hund.

____

2 Tom repariert im Moment sein Fahrrad.

____

3 Meine Eltern schlafen gerade. Sei bitte ruhig!

____

4 Ich räume im Moment mein Zimmer auf.

____

5 Wir helfen gerade unseren Eltern in der Küche.

____

max. **5**

Weniger als 4 Punkte? Wenn ja, arbeite bitte die Aufgaben 1 bis 3 nochmals durch!

C Die Verneinung

1 – I hope you**'re not watching** TV again, Elvira.
– No, I**'m not watching** TV, Mum. I'm reading, actually.

2 Where's Spooky? He**'s not/isn't playing** on the beds, is he?

♦ Um die verneinte Form des *present progressive* zu bilden, fügen wir einfach *not* hinzu, und zwar unmittelbar vor die *-ing*-Form.

4 Setze die Aussagesätze unten in die verneinte Form um.
Du kannst dabei die Langform von *be* benutzen.

1 Tom is playing with Spooky.

He is not playing with Tweets.

2 Sally and Elvira are waiting at the bus-stop.

They ____________________________ at the station.

3 Mr Nunn is cleaning his car.

He ____________________________ his bicycle.

4 We are listening to Freddy's new cassette.

We ______________________________ CD-player.

5 I am making my bed.

I ______________________________ Tom's bed.

6 You are putting away your jeans.

You ______________________________ T-shirt.

D Fragen

1 What **are you doing,** Bob? **Are you making** your bed?
2 **Is Spooky playing** in the garden?

♦ Um Fragen zu bilden, tauschen *am/is/are* und das Subjekt des Verbs ihren Platz:

Aussage: Spooky **is** playing in the garden.

Frage: **Is** Spooky playing in the garden?

5 Setze die Aussagesätze unten in die Frageform um.

1 Tom is playing football.

Is Tom playing football?

2 You are helping Dad in the garden.

______________________________ Dad in the garden?

3 Elvira is wearing her new dress.

______________________________ her new dress?

4 Miss Jolly and Mr Carter are sitting in the café.

______________________________ in the café?

5 I am playing basketball for Green Park School an Saturday.

______________________________ basketball for the school on Saturday?

6 We are doing a German test now.

______________________________?

7 Freddy is eating toffees again.

______________________________?

6 In dieser Aufgabe kommen alle drei Satzformen des *present progressive* gemischt vor. In die Fragesätze mußt du noch ein persönliches Pronomen (Fürwort) mit einsetzen.

✔ = richtig; ✗ = falsch.

bark – ~~do~~ – do – do – find – go – listen – make – play – practise – stand – talk – try – try

✔ *Elvira* What are you doing at the moment, Sally?

Sally Well, I ______________ in the hall *(Diele)*, actually. I ______________ to you on the phone.

Elvira Ha, ha. Very funny.

Sally OK. Well, I ______________ my homework, of course. ______________ it, too?

Elvira Well, I ______________ to do it, but ______________ it very difficult. But what about Tom?

Sally Oh, Tom! He ______________ to some LPs with Bob.

Elvira What? ______________ those new dances?

Sally I don't know. They ______________ an awful noise, though. Poor Mum ______________ to sleep, but she can't. Oh dear, and now Spooky ______________ at the boys. He thinks they ______________ with him.

Elvira Oh, that's bad. ______________ upstairs to stop him?

Sally Yes. Bye, Elvira.

max. 13

Weniger als 10 Punkte? Wenn ja, arbeite bitte die Aufgaben 4 bis 6 nochmals durch!

E Das *simple present* und das *present progressive* im Vergleich

1 – Come on, Tom, **I often help** you with your work. Now **I'm cleaning** the kitchen and what are you doing? Nothing.

2 – Yes, I am. **I'm keeping** Spooky's chair warm for him.

♦ Im Englischen – anders als im Deutschen – gibt es zwei Formen der Gegenwart. **Es ist nicht egal, welche Form benutzt wird.**

♦ Wir benutzen das *simple present* um auszudrücken, daß etwas immer oder immer wieder, also sehr regelmäßig, passiert; wir benutzen das *present progressive,* um etwas zu beschreiben, was im Moment des Sprechens oder Schreibens wirklich im Gange ist.

7 Setze die richtige Form der Gegenwart der angegebenen Verben in die Sätze ein.

✔ = richtig; ✗ = falsch.

✔ 1 – Look, Tom is winning (win) the race now. Bob ______ ______ (not run) very fast at the moment.

– That ______ (be) funny. Usually Bob ______ (run) much faster than Tom.

I ______ (think) he ______ (not try).

– You ______ (be) right. It ______ (be) Tom's birthday today. Bob ______ (want) to give him a nice surprise.

2 – ______ (you/tidy) your room, Elvira, or ______ (you/play) with my make-up again?

– I ______ (tidy) my room, Mum, and I never ______ (play) with make-up. I ______ (put) it on my face.

3 Elvira ______ (not do) very well at school at the moment. She ______ (become) really lazy. She never ______ (do) her homework properly, and sometimes she ______ (forget) her books. Often she ______ ______ (not wear) the school uniform, and ______ (come) to school in her disco clothes. Miss Jolly ______ (get) very worried about her at present.

max. **20**

Hast du weniger als 14 Punkte? Wenn ja, arbeite bitte die Aufgaben nochmals durch!

What are they doing?

Unser Fotograf hat leider die Bilder in einem zu dunklen Raum aufgenommen.
Kannst du trotzdem erkennen, was die Leute machen und womit?
Die Kennbuchstaben bilden den Namen einer berühmten Person.
Wer ist es?

The name of the famous person is ______________________.

7

A Form

[1] Sally **played** basketball last Saturday.
[2] Mrs Nunn **went** on holiday to Brighton three years ago.
[3] We **saw** a great film last night.

♦ Bei der Bildung des *simple past* mußt du zwischen zwei Arten von Verben unterscheiden: den **regelmäßigen** und den **unregelmäßigen** Verben.

♦ Bei den **regelmäßigen Verben** hängst du ein *-ed* an den Infinitiv an und zwar bei allen Personen [1].

♦ Die **unregelmäßigen Verben** dagegen haben eine eigene Form, die du einfach auswendig lernen mußt [2] [3]:

go ► **went**

♦ Ganz so einfach ist es mit dem Anhängen von *-ed* allerdings nicht. Es gibt bestimmte Schreibregeln, die du beachten mußt:

- Ein stummes *-e* fällt weg:
  bak**e** ► baked
  phon**e** ► phoned
- Das *-y* nach einem Konsonanten wird zum *-i*:
  carr**y** ► carr**i**ed
- Die Buchstaben *-b, -d, -m, -p, -s* und *-t* verdoppeln sich nach einem einfachen Vokal:
  dro**p** ► dro**pp**ed

1 Unterstreiche alle Verben, die im *simple past* stehen. Zeichne dann eine Tabelle auf ein Blatt Papier, wie unten vorgegeben, und trage die Verben in die richtige Spalte ein.

Tom and Sally always go to school with Bob Pratt. One day last week Bob was not at school. In the afternoon, Tom phoned Bob's mother.

Tom Hello, Mrs Pratt. Tom here. Is Bob there?

Mrs Pratt Oh, hello, Tom dear. No, Bob isn't here, I'm afraid. He's in hospital. His father is in hospital, too.

Tom What? In hospital? What happened?

Mrs Pratt Oh well, you see, Bob wanted to clean his bedroom window yesterday. First, he fetched the ladder, and then he put it against the wall and climbed up it. His dad helped him, of course. And do you know what happened then? He dropped the bucket *(Eimer)* of water on his dad's head. His dad shouted, and Bob fell off the ladder. I called an ambulance. It came very quickly, thank heavens. The doctor looked at Bob and his dad. He said, "Well, you're lucky. We have two empty beds in the hospital." Then they drove them to hospital, and that's where they are now.

Infinitiv	Imperfekt	
	-*ed*-Form (regelmäßig)	unregelmäßig
phone	phoned	was
be		

B Gebrauch

1 Bob Pratt **lived** in Liverpool **when he was a baby.**
2 His parents **moved** to Kingston **in 1979.**
3 They **bought** a house in Oak Lane **four years ago.**

♦ Wir benutzen das *simple past* für abgeschlossene Handlungen in der Vergangenheit.

♦ Der Zeitpunkt der Handlung bzw. des Vorganges wird meistens durch Zeitadverbien wie *when he was a baby, in 1979, four years ago* usw. ausgedrückt.
Weitere Signalwörter sind: *yesterday, last week/month/year/..., at 5 o'clock/10.30/...* (wenn es eindeutig später ist) usw.

2 Setze die angegebenen Verben in die Sätze ein.
Paß dabei gut auf, da die meisten davon unregelmäßig sind.

✔ = richtig; ✗ = falsch.

✔ 1 The children made (make) a big sandcastle on the beach last summer.

2 It ______ (rain) yesterday, so we ______ (stay) at home and ______ (play) indoor games.

3 Last night we ______ (see) a good programme on TV.

4 Yesterday Tom's uncle from America ______ (come) for two weeks.

5 Last summer the Carters ______ (buy) a new car.

6 Yesterday I ______ (know) the answer but now I don't.

7 In the 1850s a lot of Irish people ______ (go) to the USA because there ______ (be) no work in Ireland.

8 In the 1984 Olympic Games I ______ (do) my best but I ______ (be) still last.

9 Axel ______ (write) a letter to his father last week.

10 We ______ (see) snow on the mountains last summer.

max. 13

Weniger als 10 Punkte? Wenn ja, arbeite bitte die Aufgaben 1 und 2 nochmals durch!

C Fragen

Ein Polizist stellt Fragen über einen Unfall.

	Frage-wort	Hilfs-verb	Subjekt	Voll-verb	Objekt	andere Satzteile
1		**Did**	you	**see**	the accident,	madam?
2	Where	**did**	the duck	**run**		in front of the car?
3		**Did**	the red sports car	**come**		along the road too fast?

♦ Erinnerst du dich? Fragen in dem *simple past* werden mit *did* gebildet, wenn kein anderes Hilfsverb im Satz vorhanden ist. Das Vollverb steht dann im Infinitiv.

3 Schau dir die Personen auf Seite 61 an. Sie erinnern sich an das, was sie gestern gemacht haben.
Stelle nun die Fragen, die zu den Bildern passen.

1 Freddy *Did Freddy read a book?*

2 Mr Carter ______________________________?

3 Miss Jolly ______________________________?

4 Bob ______________________________?

5 Sally ______________________________?

6 Elvira ______________________________?

7 Tom ______________________________?

8 Mrs Nunn ______________________________?

1

read/book
FREDDY

2

take/bus
MRCARTER

3

buy/dress
MISS JOLLY

4

go/bed/9 o'clock
BOB

5

do/washing-up
SALLY

6

clean/room
ELVIRA

7

repair / bicycle
TOM

8

have/day's holiday
MRS NUNN

4 Stelle Fragen nach den unterstrichenen Satzteilen.
Benutze die folgenden Fragewörter: *when? where? what? who? how?*

1 Miss Jolly lived in Bonn in 1980.

✔ When did Miss Jolly live in Bonn?

2 Last summer Tom went to Spain.

_______________ last summer?

3 Yesterday I played volleyball.

_______ you _______ yesterday?

4 Spooky ran after the Brown's cat last weekend.

Who _______________ last weekend?

5 We watched a film at school today.

_______ you _______ at school today?

6 Elvira saw a famous pop star on Monday.

_______________?

7 Sally caught a cold because she didn't wear a coat.

How _______________?

max. 6

Weniger als 5 Punkte? Wenn ja, arbeite bitte die Aufgaben 3 und 4 nochmals durch!

D Die Verneinung

Hier sind die Antworten auf die Fragen des Polizisten über den Unfall (siehe Seite 60):

Subjekt	Hilfs-verb	Voll-verb	Objekt	andere Satzteile
1 I	**didn't**	**see**	the accident.	
2 The duck	**didn't**	**run**		in front of the car.
3 The sports car	**didn't**	**come**		along the road too fast.

♦ Wenn kein anderes Hilfsverb im Satz vorhanden ist, werden Vollverben im *simple past* mit *did not/didn't* verneint. Das Vollverb steht dabei im Infinitiv.

5 Verneine bitte folgende Sätze.

1 I saw the police car.
I didn't see the accident.

2 My mother phoned the police.
I ______

3 A duck ran in front of the car.
A dog ______

4 The blue car came too quickly.
The red car ______

5 The red car stopped in time *(rechtzeitig)*.
The blue car ______

6 A reporter came to the accident.
An ambulance ______

7 The driver of the blue car took a taxi.
The driver of the red car ______

6 Übersetze die unterstrichenen Satzteile ins Englische.
Paß dabei gut auf, da alle Formen des *simple past* vorkommen.

✔ = richtig; ✗ = falsch.

1 Gestern kam unser Onkel aus Amerika zum Mittagessen.

Er gab mir ein schönes Buch über New York.

2 – Bist du vor zwei Tagen ins Kino gegangen?

– Nein, ich bin nicht ins Kino gegangen.

Ich bin mit meinen Eltern ins Theater gegangen.

3 Elvira tanzte in einem Tanzwettbewerb *(dancing competition)* am Wochenende.

Sie hat aber nicht gewonnen.

4 Miss Jolly und Mr Carter trafen sich nochmals gestern abend.

Tom sah sie in der Stadt.

max. 9

Weniger als 7 Punkte? Wenn ja, arbeite bitte die Aufgaben 5 und 6 nochmals durch!

Sally and the ghost

A mixed-up sentence story

Die 11 Sätze dieser Geschichte sind in die falsche Reihenfolge geraten. Benutze Zahlen von 1 bis 11, um die Geschichte sinnvoll wiederherzustellen.

- ○ On the first night, Sally suddenly woke up.
- ○ Then the thing suddenly jumped on to her bed.
- (1) The Cobbs went to Scotland on holiday last summer.
- ○ Then Sally screamed, and the thing started to bark happily.
- ○ They stayed in an old castle near Inverness.
- ○ After hearing the noise, she lay in bed, too frightened to move.
- ○ Everything was dark.
- ○ The thing moved across the bed towards her face.
- ○ She waited for the noise to come again.
- ○ It was just Spooky.
- ○ Then she heard a noise: there was someone, or something, in her bedroom.

8

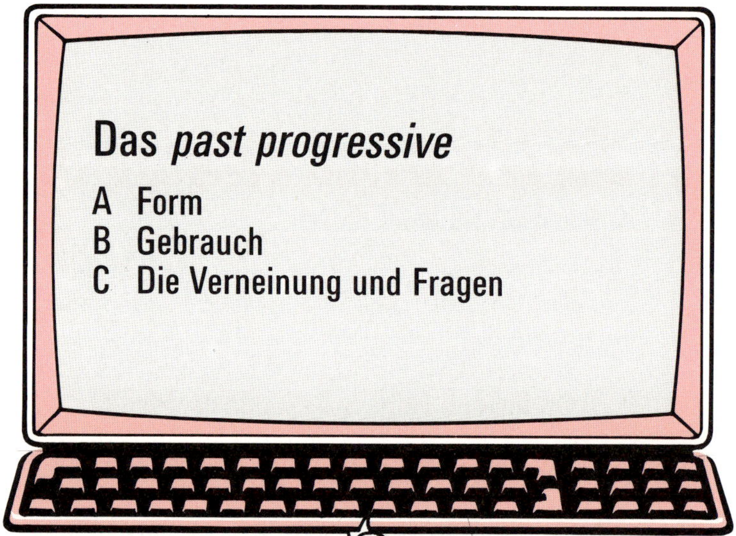

A Form

1 When Sally phoned, Bob **was watching** TV and Mrs Pratt **was cooking** the supper.

2 The children **were talking** when Mr Carter came in.

♦ Wir bilden das *past progressive* mit *was/were* + der *-ing*-Form des Vollverbs:

	bejaht	verneint
	Langform	Langform/Kurzform
I	was watching	was not/wasn't watching
you	were cooking	were not/weren't cooking
he	was helping	was not/wasn't helping
she	was making	was not/wasn't making
it	was running	was not/wasn't running
we	were eating	were not/weren't eating
you	were playing	were not/weren't playing
they	were working	were not/weren't working

1 Gestern nachmittag gab es in Kingston große Aufregung. Ein Flugzeug stürzte in der Nähe der Stadt ab. Sieh dir die Bilder unten an und sage, was die Personen gerade taten, als der Unfall passierte.

1 Mr Pratt was washing his car.

2 Elvira ______________________________ her room.

3 Sally and her friends ______________________________.

4 Mrs Nunn ______________________________ work.

5 Mr and Mrs Cobb ______________________________ in the garden.

6 Mrs Clarke ______________________________ tea,

and Freddy ______________________________.

7 ______________________________

______________________________.

B Gebrauch

1 Elvira **was practising** the guitar when Sally **telephoned.**
2 Spooky and Coco **were playing** when Tom **came** home.

♦ Das *past progressive* wird benutzt, um auszudrücken, daß irgendetwas schon im Gange war, als eine andere Tätigkeit einsetzte:

Elvira **was practising** the guitar … → … when Sally **telephoned.**

♦ Im Deutschen gibt es keine *progressive*-Form, daher benutzen wir Ausdrücke wie „gerade“:

- Spooky and Coco **were playing** when Tom came home.
  Spooky und Coco **spielten gerade,** als Tom nach Hause kam.

♦ Es gibt keine eindeutigen Signalwörter, die dir helfen, zu entscheiden, ob du das *past progressive* benutzen sollst.
Wenn es aber zwei (oder mehrere) Vorgänge gibt, die **gleichzeitig** geschehen, sollst du überlegen:

- kommt ein Vorgang „plötzlich dazwischen“?
  Wenn ja, mußt du dafür das *past simple* benutzen. Sehr häufig werden solche plötzlich auftretenden Vorgänge von den Adverbien *when, as* oder *suddenly* begleitet.

2 Setze die angegebenen Verben in die richtige Form des *simple past* oder des *past progressive* ein.

✔ = richtig; ✗ = falsch.

1 When Miss Jolly ______ (walk) into the room, the children ______ (sit) at their desks. Some of them ______ (read) and others ______ (do) their project work. Bob and Sally ______ (talk) to Elvira. She ______ (plan) the youth club party. And Freddy? He ______ (eat), of course. He ______ (eat) two bags of toffees yesterday.

2 We ______ (see) something funny today. A horrible man in a sports car ______ (come)

along the road too fast when an old lady suddenly ________ ______________ (start) to cross the road. The man ______________ (try) to stop. He ______________ (miss) the lady, but he ______________ (hit) another car that ______________ (drive) the other way. The man ______________ (be) unlucky because a policeman ______________ (sit) in the car. When we ______________ (go) away, the policeman ______________ (write) the man's name into his book, and everyone else ______________ (laugh).

max. **20**

Weniger als 15 Punkte? Wenn ja, arbeite bitte die Aufgaben 1 und 2 nochmals durch!

C Die Verneinung und Fragen

1 Sally **wasn't dancing** when Bob came. She was talking to Elvira.
2 **Were** you **helping** your mum all day on Saturday?

♦ Um einen Satz zu verneinen, fügen wir einfach das Wörtchen *not* unmittelbar nach *was/were* ein.

♦ Um eine Frage zu bilden, tauschen wir das Subjekt des Satzes und das Hilfsverb *was/were* aus, genau wie im Deutschen.

3 Bilde jeweils zwei Sätze, wie in dem Beispiel unten vorgegeben.

1 (play handball/play football)

Tom *was not (wasn't) playing handball* on Saturday.

He *was playing football*.

2 (do cooking/do cleaning)

Sally ______________ the cooking yesterday.

She ______________.

3 (clean car/clean windows)

The Cobbs ______________________ the car when I saw them. They ______________________.

4 (practise guitar/practise piano)

I ______________________ the guitar when you telephoned. I ______________________.

5 (be silly/work)

Tom and Freddy ______________ ______________ silly in Maths yesterday. They ______________ ______________ hard all the time.

6 (do/have)

We ______________________ our homework when Elvira came round. We ______________________ tea.

4 Benutze die unterstrichenen Satzteile, um Fragen mit *what? where? when?* und *who?* zu stellen.

1 Where was Tom playing football?

Tom was playing football in the park.

2 ______________________ German words?

Sally was learning her German words last night.

3 ______________________ all evening?

Bob and Elvira were dancing at the youth club all evening.

4 ______________________ all afternoon?

Bob was helping Miss Jolly all afternoon.

5 ______________________ in the midday break?

I was doing my homework in the midday break.

6 ______________________ 10 o'clock?

Mrs Nunn was working till 10 o'clock on Wednesday.

5 Dies ist eine gemischte Übung, in der alle Personen und Formen, also auch verneinte Sätze und Fragen, des *past progressive* vorkommen. Setze die angegebenen Verben ein.

✔ = richtig; ✗ = falsch.

1 Sally ______________________ (not play) basketball last Saturday.
She ______________________ (practise) for the dancing competition.

2 Tom Cobb, ______________________ (you/talk) to Bob again?

3 The Oak Lane children ______________________ (camp) in the garden all last weekend.

4 You're wrong. Mr and Mrs Nunn ______________________ (not bake) cakes yesterday.
They ______________________ (make) bread.

5 ______________________ (she/laugh) at Elvira? – Oh, no.
Mr Carter ______________________ (tell) her a joke.

6 Don't be silly. Spooky and Coco ______________________ (not be) naughty. They ______________________ (play), that's all.

7 ______________________ (you/do) your homework when I phoned?

8 – What ______________________ (you/do) this time yesterday?
– Oh, I ______________________ (take) Spooky for a walk.

9 Tom ran into the tree because he ______________________ (not look) where he ______________________ (go).
He ______________________ (tease) Freddy all the time.

max. 16

Weniger als 12 Punkte? Wenn ja, arbeite bitte die Aufgaben 3 bis 5 nochmals durch!

Who was doing what?

Wer ist der Dieb? Inspektor Sperrick von Scotland Yard befragt alle Leute, was sie gestern abend um 10 Uhr machten, als der Einbruch passierte. Einer lügt. Wer ist es?
Vervollständige die Sätze mit den richtigen Verben und stelle die Unstimmigkeiten fest.

Billy I ______________________ a bath.
Fred We ______________________ books at home.
Larry I ______________________ Bessy.
Peter I ______________________ a film at the cinema.
Sally I ______________________ a beer at the pub.
Sam I ______________________ cards with Larry Lamb.
Cat/Dirty We ______________________ home in the rain.
Bessy I ______________________ to Larry on the phone.
Mack I ______________________ my supper.

The thief was ______________ because ______________

____.

9

A Form

1 Tom **has finished** his homework. He can go out now.
2 **I've washed** the car, Dad. It looks great.
3 Sally **hasn't cleaned** Tweets's cage *(Käfig)* yet.
4 **Have** you **done** your Maths, Tom?

♦ Wir bilden das *present perfect* im Englischen immer mit *have/has* + Partizip (3. Form). Im Deutschen dagegen benutzen wir „haben" und „sein". Im Englischen sieht das *present perfect* also wie folgt aus:

	bejaht		verneint	
	Langform/Kurzform		Langform/Kurzform	
I	have/'ve	finished	have not/haven't	finished
you	have/'ve	washed	have not/haven't	washed
he	has/'s	turned	has not/hasn't	turned
she	has/'s	cleaned	has not/hasn't	cleaned
it	has/'s	played	has not/hasn't	played
we	have/'ve	made	have not/haven't	made
you	have/'ve	bought	have not/haven't	bought
they	have/'ve	been	have not/haven't	been

♦ Bei **regelmäßigen Verben** wird das Partizip aus dem Infinitiv + *-ed* gebildet. Es ist die gleiche Form wie die des *simple past:*
play + -ed ▸ play**ed**

♦ Ganz so einfach ist es bei dem Anhängen von *-ed* aber auch nicht. Du mußt bei manchen Verben besondere Schreibregeln beachten:

phon**e**	▸ phoned:	ein stummes *-e* fällt weg;
empt**y**	▸ emptied:	das *-y* nach einem Konsonant wird zum *-i* verwandelt;
dro**p**	▸ dro**pp**ed:	*-b, -d, -m, -p, -s* und *-t* werden nach einem einfachen Vokal verdoppelt.

♦ Die **unregelmäßigen Verben** haben eine eigene Form, die du einfach auswendig lernen mußt:

be ▸ **been**

Die Verneinung wird durch das Einfügen des Wörtchens *not* unmittelbar nach *have/has* gebildet [3].

♦ Um Fragen zu bilden, brauchst du nur *have/has* und das Subjekt des Satzes auszutauschen [4].

1 Unterstreiche zunächst in der folgenden Geschichte alle Verben, die im *present perfect* stehen.

T So, that's it! I've worked enough. I'm going out.

S What, you're going out? But you haven't finished your work yet.

T Did you say I haven't finished? Look, I've washed the car, I've mended the radio and I've cleaned the garage. Haven't I done enough? There isn't anything else to do anyway.

S Oh yes, there is, Tom. You haven't taken the rubbish *(Abfall)* out yet and you haven't written to Aunt Mary. You haven't thanked her for your birthday present.

T OK, OK, Sally. But the sun's shining. It's rained all week and this is the first dry day. I want to go out with my friends. I haven't been out all week.

S Poor old Tom! Anyhow, what about your school work? We're having a German test tomorrow, and you haven't done any work for it at all.

T What do you mean? Bob and I have learnt all the words Miss Jolly gave us. Wait and see, I'll get top marks.

2 Setze die angegebenen Verben ins *present perfect*.
Paß dabei gut auf, da alle Verben unregelmäßig sind.

1 Miss Jolly ____________________ (go) home. She's ill.

2 Tom and Bob ____________________ (be) away a long time. Are they all right?

3 Sally ____________________ (feed) Spooky. No more food for him!

4 I ____________________ (not do) all the cleaning.

5 Mrs Nunn ____________________ (give) Elvira a lovely new dress.

6 Give me those sweets, Freddy. You ____________________ (eat) a whole bag of toffees already.

7 Look at the boys' homework! They ____________________ (make) a lot of mistakes.

8 Tom, I ____________________ (tell) you to stop talking three times already. Come and see me at the end of the lesson.

B Allgemeiner Gebrauch

1 Sally's a good girl. She **has done** her homework, **tidied** her room and got the tea ready.
2 Tom and Bob are ill. They **have caught** a cold *(sich eine Erkältung geholt)*.
3 **I've bought** a lovely new dress. Do you want to see it?

♦ In den Sätzen oben hören wir irgendetwas über die Vergangenheit, **ohne aber den genauen Zeitpunkt des Geschehens zu erfahren.**

♦ Wenn wir sagen, daß jemand etwas getan hat oder daß etwas geschehen ist – **nicht aber, wann es sich ereignet hat** – benutzen wir das *present perfect*.

3 Schreibe Sätze wie in dem Beispielsatz vorgegeben.
Benutze durchweg das *present perfect*.

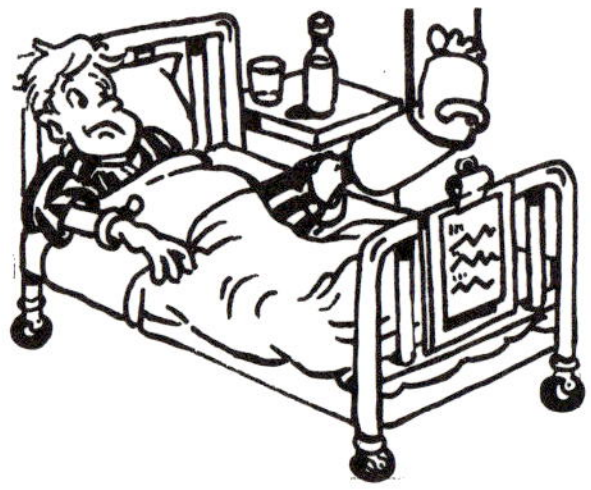

1 Tom is in hospital.

✔ He has broken his leg.

(break/leg)

2 Sally and Elvira are happy.

____

___________________________________.

(do/their homework)

3 Mr Clarke is proud *(stolz)*.

____

___________________________________.

(buy/new car)

4 Mr and Mrs Pratt are glad.

____

___________________________________.

(finish/garden)

5 Freddy is ill.

____

___________________________________.

(eat/too many toffees)

6 We are brown because we

____

______________________.

(be/on holiday)

max.
5

Weniger als 3 Punkte? Wenn ja, arbeite bitte die Aufgaben 1 bis 3 nochmals durch!

Ⓒ Gebrauch mit gewissen Zeitadverbien

1 – **Have** you **finished** your homework **yet**, Tom?
– **I've just finished** my English, but I **haven't done** my Maths **yet**.

2 – **Have** you **ever been** to Scotland?
– No, **we have never been** to Scotland, but we'**ve been** to England.

♦ Oft benutzen wir das *present perfect,* um eine Handlung bzw. einen Zustand zu beschreiben, die/der in der Vergangenheit angefangen hat, aber in die Gegenwart hineinreicht.

♦ Der genaue Zeitpunkt in der Vergangenheit wird nicht genannt. Nur das gegenwärtige **Ergebnis** interessiert uns.

♦ Deshalb treten folgende Zeitadverbien häufig mit dem *present perfect* zusammen auf.
Sie gelten also als Signalwörter für das *present perfect*:

just – *gerade*
already – *schon*
yet – *bis jetzt*
not yet – *bis jetzt noch nicht*
ever – *jemals*
never – *bisher noch nie*

4 Benutze die unten angegebenen Satzelemente, um Sätze mit dem *present perfect* zu bilden.

1 Tom has just gone (just/go) home.

2 We ______________________ (already/do) this exercise.

3 Tom and Sally ______________________ (not yet/finish) cleaning their rooms.

4 __________ you ______________________ (ever/see) a lion?

5 Mr Carter ______________________ (never/be) to Wales.

6 I ______________________ (just/buy) a new pen.

7 __________ Sally and Elvira ______________________ (already/see) this film?

8 Freddy Clarke ______________________ (already/eat) two bags of toffees today.

D Das *present perfect* und das *simple past* im Vergleich

1 Tom **has broken** his leg. He **broke** it yesterday.
2 I **have bought** a great record. I **bought** it last Saturday.

♦ Wir verwenden das *simple past,* wenn wir sagen wollen, **wann** jemand etwas in der Vergangenheit getan hat oder **wann** etwas in der Vergangenheit geschah *(yesterday, in 1970, last week, ...).*

♦ Wir benutzen das *present perfect,* wenn wir über das gegenwärtige **Ergebnis** einer Handlung bzw. eines Zustandes sprechen wollen.

5 Versehe die richtige Form des Verbs mit einem Haken.

1 The Cobbs ... a new car last week.
☐ have bought
☐ bought

2 Oh, look! That car ... an accident.
☐ has just had
☐ just had

3 Tom, ... your homework yet?
- have you done
- did you do

4 Mr Carter ... some roses for Miss Jolly yesterday.
- has bought
- bought

5 Last summer Tom ... climbing in Wales.
- has gone
- went

6 Most people ... a marathon.
- have never run
- never ran

6 Setze die angegebenen Verben ins *present perfect* oder *simple past* ein.

✔ = richtig; ✗ = falsch.

1 Yesterday Tom ____________ (go) to school by bike. He ____________ (meet) Bob at school. 'There's a new film at the cinema, "Moonbusters". Do you want to go at the weekend?' he ____________ (ask) Bob.
'No, I ____________ (see) it already. I ____________ (see) it last month when I ____________ (be) on holiday in Manchester.'
'I ____________ (not see) it,' ____________ (say) Sally. 'The last film I ____________ (see) ____________ (be) "E.T.".'
'Well, we ____________ (win) four free tickets to the cinema and Mum ____________ (give) them to me.'

2 'Bob, ____________ (you/see) Gilda or Freddy yet?' 'Well, I ____________ (not see) Gilda, but I ____________ (see) Freddy. He ____________ (go) into the sweet shop to buy some toffees. Look there he is. He's eating, as usual.'

max. **16**

Weniger als 12 Punkte? Wenn ja, arbeite bitte die Aufgaben 4 bis 6 nochmals durch!

A lettersquare

Die 3. Form (Partizip) der 15 unten aufgelisteten Verben ist in dem *Lettersquare* versteckt. 5 davon sind normal (►), 2 von rechts nach links (◄), 5 von oben nach unten (▼) und 3 diagonal (►,◄) geschrieben. Kannst du die 15 Verbformen finden?

Die Verben im Infinitiv:

~~be~~ – begin – build – catch – cut – do – draw – eat – forget – grow – know – lend – mean – ride – teach

T	H	G	U	A	T	F	A	T	Q	I	O	U	B	J
C	V	A	C	A	U	G	H	T	R	D	C	L	E	E
G	C	H	B	B	R	K	V	U	R	I	F	D	G	W
E	Q	T	U	F	P	L	E	N	T	C	D	B	Q	P
S	N	I	S	E	K	G	Z	T	R	N	O	D	X	N
O	L	G	X	H	S	B	A	D	E	O	N	M	E	Y
T	W	R	A	E	O	B	Q	K	Z	L	E	D	M	N
L	E	Z	Y	E	**B**	**E**	**E**	**N**	T	M	E	A	N	T
P	A	H	I	Y	T	G	S	O	N	L	Y	I	Z	O
M	T	F	U	X	C	U	T	W	X	C	H	D	E	R
G	E	R	Y	B	L	N	I	N	D	X	X	O	G	M
I	N	H	Q	P	J	L	O	M	H	R	P	G	R	A
K	V	B	E	N	A	J	W	I	V	A	A	C	O	W
K	U	G	B	U	J	D	P	H	Q	B	U	W	W	L
N	E	T	T	O	G	R	O	F	S	K	I	D	N	A

10

Ⓐ Das *going to-future*

1 I **am going to have** a party next Friday.

2 Elvira **is going to buy** a new dress.

3 We **are going to go swimming** later.

♦ Wir bilden das *going to-future* wie folgt:

Subjekt	*be*	*going to*	Infinitiv	andere Satzteile
I	am	going to	have	a party next Friday.
Elvira	is	going to	buy	a new dress.
We	are	going to	go	swimming later.

♦ Wir benutzen das *going to-future,* wenn wir über zukünftige Pläne und Vorhaben sprechen möchten.

1 Die Oak Lane-Kinder und ihre Eltern und Lehrer planen ihr Wochenende.
Sage, was die Personen am Wochenende vorhaben. Benutze das *going to-future*.

1 Mr Carter is going to wash his car.

2 Elvira ______________________ in a disco.

3 Sally ______________________ basketball.

4 The Cobbs ______________________ in the garden.

5 The Pratts ______________________ the kitchen.

6 Mrs Nunn ______________________ her bus.

B Das *will-future*

1 Spooky **will be** three years old on November 18th.
2 Don't eat so many toffees. You **will get** fat.
3 Mr Carter **won't be** angry with you. He'**ll be** nice.

♦ Wir bilden das *will-future* wie folgt:

	bejaht	verneint
	Lang-/Kurzform	Lang-/Kurzform
I	will/'ll see	will not/won't see
you	will/'ll see	will not/won't see
he/she/it	will/'ll see	will not/won't see
we	will/'ll see	will not/won't see
you	will/'ll see	will not/won't see
they	will/'ll see	will not/won't see

♦ Wir benutzen das *will-future,* um über zukünftige Vorgänge, auf die wir keinen Einfluß haben, zu sprechen 1.

♦ Wir benutzen das *will-future* auch, um eine Vorhersage zu machen oder eine Vermutung zu äußern 2 3.

2 Setze die angegebenen Verben ein.
Benutze dabei nur das *will-future,* und zwar in der Langform.

1 I will see (see) you at the youth club tonight, Sally.
2 Take a coat. It ______________________ (rain) soon.
3 Bob ______________________ (not play) football this week. He's ill.
4 The teachers ______________________ (be) at the form party.
5 Elvira ______________________ (not come) to school without her uniform again. She ______________________ (get) into trouble.
6 We ______________________ (miss) the train. We must go now.

3 Benutze das *will-* bzw. das *going to-future,* um die Sätze mit den angegebenen Verben zu vervollständigen.

✔ = richtig; ✗ = falsch.

✔ 1 What *will happen* (happen) if Tom is late again?

✔ 2 Bob *is going to have* (have) a party on his birthday.

3 Elvira ______________________ (be) 14 tomorrow.

4 I ______________________ (not buy) Freddy any more sweets. I ______________________ (give) him apples.

5 Freddy ______________________ (get) toothache from all those sweets.

6 Spooky ________________ (not bark) if you take him out.

7 Tweets has no water and no food. Be careful, or she ______________ (be) ill and she ______________ (die).

8 Mr Carter ____________________ (give) us a test on Friday.

9 They are building a big new road in Kingston. Soon it __________________ (be) very noisy in Oak Lane.

10 The Nunns ______________________ (get) a bigger flat.

max. 10

Weniger als 7 Punkte? Wenn ja, arbeite bitte die Aufgaben 1 bis 3 nochmals durch!

What are they going to be?

Was möchten diese Jugendlichen werden, wenn sie älter sind?
Leider hat der Schreibcomputer hier verrückt gespielt.
Kannst du die Berufe trotzdem erkennen?

1	Tom	ECRETAH
2	Freddy	POHSEPREKE
3	Elvira	CRANDE
4	Dirk and Colin	NASCHICEM
5	Jane	XATI-RIDREV
6	Peter	TEV
7	Sally and Sue	RUSENS
8	Bob	RATS ALRELBOTOF
9	Ann	TIDNETS

1 Tom is going to be a teacher.

2 Freddy is going to be a s____________________.

3 Elvira is going to _______________ d_______________.

4 Dirk and Colin are going to be m____________________.

5 Jane ____________________ t_______________.

6 Peter ____________________ v_______________.

7 Sally and Sue are going to be n____________________.

8 Bob ____________________________________.

9 Ann ____________________________________.

11

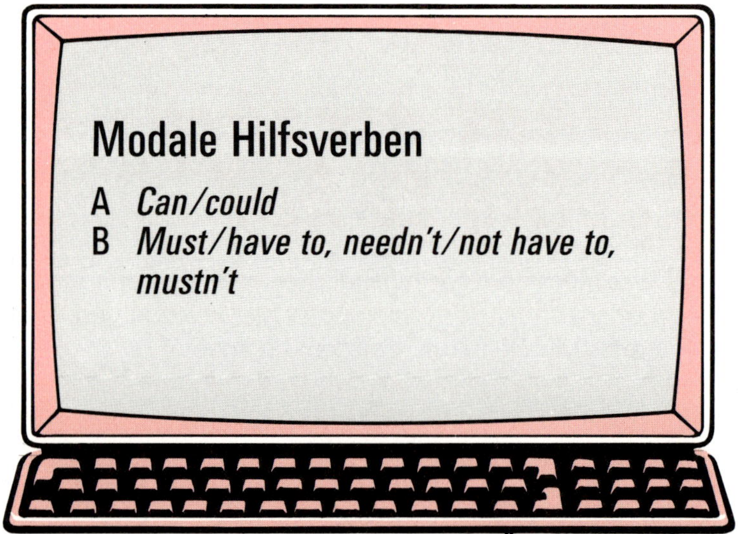

Modale Hilfsverben

A *Can/could*
B *Must/have to, needn't/not have to, mustn't*

A Can/could

1	Tom **can** swim well. He **could** swim when he was five years old.
2	You **can't** go home yet, but you **can** put your things away.
3	The doctor said I **could** see Mrs Nunn for just two minutes. She's very ill.

♦ Das Hilfsverb *can* kommt nur in der Gegenwart *(present)* und der Vergangenheit *(past)* vor. Alle Personen haben die gleiche Form:

Gegenwart		Vergangenheit	
bejaht	verneint	bejaht	verneint
can	cannot/can't	could	could not/couldn't

♦ Genau wie bei „können" im Deutschen, benutzen wir *can/could,* um Fähigkeit 1 und Erlaubnis 2 3 auszudrücken.

♦ *Can/could* können nicht alleine stehen. Sie müssen immer ein Vollverb bei sich haben:

- My sister **can speak** French.
  Meine Schwester **kann** Französisch.

1 Sieh dir die Tabelle an und benutze *can/can't,* um zu sagen, welche Tätigkeiten Mr und Mrs Cobb können bzw. nicht tun können.

	speak German	drive a car	bake a cake	swim	repair a chair
Mr Cobb	✗	✓	✗	✗	✓
Mrs Cobb	✗	✓	✓	✓	✗

1 Mr Cobb can't speak German, ______________ a cake or ______________, but he ______________ a car and ______________ a chair.

2 Mrs Cobb ______________ German or ______________ a chair, but she ______________ a car, ______________ a cake and ______________.

2 Beantworte die folgenden Fragen mit *yes.* Dann frage nochmal und antworte mit *no,* aber diesmal alles in der Vergangenheit.

1 Can Miss Jolly drive a car?

Yes, she can.

Could she drive a car ten years ago?

No, she couldn't.

2 Can Freddy swim?

Yes, he ______________.

______________ when he was a baby?

No, he ______________.

3 Can Tom roller-skate?

Yes, ______________.

______________ last year?

No, he ______________.

4 Can Elvira read German well?

Yes, ______________________.

______________________________________ well three years ago?

No, she ______________________.

5 Can you ride a bike?

Yes, I ______________________.

______________________________________ when you started school?

No, ______________________.

B *Must/have to; needn't/not have to; mustn't*

1	British children	**must** **have to**	go to school from 9 to 4.
2	I	**needn't** **don't have**	to go to school tomorrow.
3	Tom **mustn't** ride his bike on the pavement.		

	Gebrauch	deutsche Entsprechung
must *have to* }	Zwang bzw. starke Notwendigkeit	müssen 1
need not/needn't *not have to* }	Kein Zwang bzw. keine Notwendigkeit	nicht brauchen/ nicht müssen 2
must not/mustn't	Verbot	nicht dürfen 3

♦ *Must, needn't* und *mustn't* können nur in der Gegenwart *(present)* verwendet werden.
Have to/not have to kann dagegen alle Zeiten bilden.

3 Setze *must* bzw. *mustn't* in die Sätze ein.

1 You __________ smoke in school.

2 You __________ wash your hands before dinner.

3 Tom, you __________ just take apples from Mrs Brown's tree. You __________ ask her first.

4 Freddy __________ eat so many toffees. He's much too fat.

5 Bob __________ miss his bus today. We __________ be at the airport by 5 o'clock.

6 Tom, you __________ forget to take Spooky for a walk. He __________ go out every day.

4 Sieh dir die Verkehrszeichen an, und setze *must* oder *have to*, *needn't* oder *don't have to* oder *mustn't* ein.

1 You *must/have to* give way here, but you *needn't/don't have to* stop if nothing is coming.

2 You __________ overtake.

3 You __________ always stop here.

4 You ______________________ turn left here.

You ______________________ turn right or go straight on.

5 You ______________________ be careful here.

6 You ______________________ go at just 30 mph any longer.

7 Lorries ______________________ overtake here, but cars ______________________ worry about this sign.

5 Sieh dir die Schilder an, und setze *can, can't, must* oder *have to, needn't* oder *don't have to* oder *mustn't* und ein geeignetes Vollverb aus der Liste unten ein.

✔ = richtig; ✗ = falsch.

be – drive – ~~eat~~ – feed – go – go – have – help – swim – use – wait

✔ 1 You mustn't eat ice-cream in the shop.

2 We ______________ feed the monkeys at 4 o'clock, but we ______________ them at 2 o'clock.

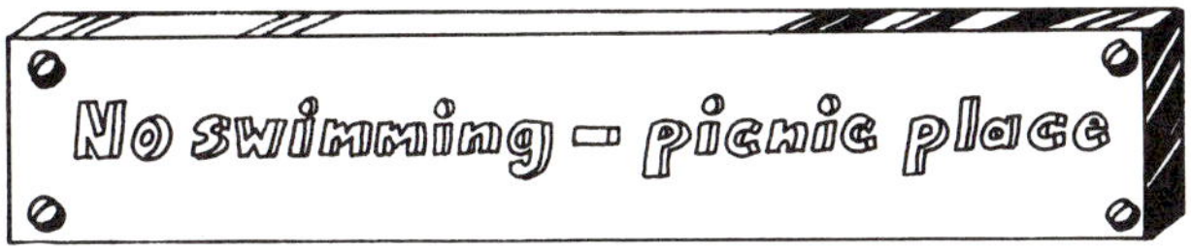

3 People ______________ here, but you ______________ a picnic if you want.

4 We ______________ quiet after 10 p.m., but we ______________ to bed.

5 Cars ______________ fast in this lane, but you ______________ it if you don't want to go so fast.

6 Children ______________ into the bar, but they ______________ in the children's room.

max. 10

Weniger als 7 Punkte? Wenn ja, arbeite die Aufgaben 1 bis 5 nochmals durch!

You mustn't do that!

Lies dir gut durch, was man machen darf und was nicht. Male dann zu jedem Satz ein geeignetes Verkehrs- bzw. Verbotsschild.

1

2

3

4

1 Big, expensive cars mustn't overtake little cars.
2 You mustn't do any homework.
3 Teachers mustn't get angry with pupils.
4 No tests.

Little Red Riding Hood

Jeder kennt das Märchen vom Rotkäppchen und dem bösen Wolf. Setze die Verben in den richtigen Zeiten ein, um diese englische Fassung zu vervollständigen.

Once upon a time there was [1] (be) a little girl, who ________ [2] (live) near a big forest. She always ________ [3] (wear) a cloak *(Umhang)* with a red hood like the cloaks that riders ________ [4] (use) so soon everyone ________ [5] (call) her Little Red Riding Hood.

One day Little Red Riding Hood's mother ________ [6] (say), 'Your grandmother ________ [7] (be) ill and she ________ [8] (lie) in bed. She ________ [9] (need) some food. Please ________ [10] (take) this basket to her. Please ________ [11] (be) quick. She ________ [12] (wait) for it.' So Little Red Riding Hood ________ [13] (put on) her cloak, ________ [14] (pick up) the basket, ________ [15] (kiss) her mother goodbye and ________ [16] (leave) the house. 'I ________ [17] (go) through the forest,' ________ [18] (think) Little Red Riding Hood. 'It ________ [19] (be) much quicker,' and she ________ [20] (go) into the big dark forest.

Little Red Riding Hood ________ [21] (walk) through the forest when suddenly a wolf ________ [22] (come) out of the trees and ________ [23] (speak) to her. 'Good morning, Little Red Riding Hood,' ________ [24] (say) the wolf. 'Where ________ [25] (you/go) to?' 'I ________ [26] (take) this basket of food to my grandmother,' she ________ [27] (answer). 'My grandmother ________ [28] (be) ill. She ________ [29] (lie) in bed. But I

__________ [30] (must/hurry). She __________ [31] (feel) hungry. She __________ [32] (wait) for her dinner.'

When the big bad wolf __________ [33] (hear) the world 'dinner', he __________ [34] (feel) hungry, too. He __________ [35] (look at) the little girl and he __________ [36] (have) an idea. The wolf __________ [37] (say) goodbye to Little Red Riding Hood and he __________ [38] (run) off into the forest.

When Little Red Riding Hood __________ [39] (arrive) at her grandmother's house, she __________ [40] (open) the door and __________ [41] (go) in. She __________ [42] (lay) the basket on the table and then __________ [43] (climb) the stairs to her grandmother's bedroom. She __________ [44] (knock) on the bedroom door. 'Come in,' __________ [45] (call) a voice. Little Red Riding Hood __________ [46] (push) the door open and __________ [47] (go) into the room. She __________ [48] (think) her grandmother __________ [49] (look) a little funny – she __________ [50] (seem) much bigger than usual. 'Hallo, grandmother,' __________ [51] (say) Little Red Riding Hood sweetly. 'How __________ [52] (you/feel) today?' 'I __________ [53] (not feel) very well,' __________ [54] (say) her grandmother. 'But why __________ [55] (you/stand) so far away from me? __________ [56] (come) nearer, dear.' So Little Red Riding Hood __________ [57] (move) closer to the bed. She __________ [58] (look) at her grandmother closely. 'What funny teeth you __________ [59] (have), dear grandmother,' she __________ [60] (say). Then the big bad wolf __________ [61] (jump) out of the bed, __________ [62] (catch) the little girl and __________ [63] (eat) her up.

The wolf __________[64] (leave) the house and __________[65] (go) home. He __________[66] (be) tired after his big dinner, so he __________[67] (want) to have a sleep.

Soon Little Red Riding Hood's mother __________[68] (become) worried. 'I __________[69] (wonder) what __________ __________[70] (happen) to her,' she __________[71] (think). 'She __________[72] (be) away too long. Perhaps she __________[73] (lose) her way in the forest. I __________[74] (go) and __________[75] (find) the forester. He __________[76] (know) what to do.'

When the forester __________[77] (hear) the mother's story he __________[78] (say), 'Ah, I __________[79] (know) what __________[80] (happen). The big bad wolf __________[81] (eat) her. But __________ __________[82] (not worry). I __________[83] (shoot) the wolf. Perhaps it __________[84] (not be) too late.' So the forester __________[85] (get) his gun and __________[86] (go) into the forest. He soon __________[87] (find) the big bad wolf and he __________[88] (kill) him. Then the forester __________[89] (take) his long knife and __________[90] (cut) the wolf open. Little Red Riding Hood and her grandmother __________[91] (climb) out of the wolf's stomach *(Bauch)*. They __________[92] (look) a little frightened, but otherwise *(sonst)* they __________[93] (be) all right.

See you again in Band II!